Tax Planning

SIXTH EDITION

By

PHILIP LAWTON, M.A., LL.M. (Cantab.)
of Lincoln's Inn, Barrister

and

ANTHONY SUMPTION
of Lincoln's Inn, Barrister

(*both formerly solicitors of the Supreme Court*)

LONDON

Oyez Publishing

OYEZ PUBLISHING LIMITED
OYEZ HOUSE, 237 LONG LANE,
LONDON SE1 4PU
1973

SBN 85120 158 X

First Published . . .	June, 1962
Reprinted . . .	August, 1962
Second Edition . . .	September, 1966
Third Edition . . .	October, 1968
Fourth Edition . . .	December, 1969
Fifth Edition . . .	December, 1971
Sixth Edition . . .	November, 1973

MADE AND PRINTED IN GREAT BRITAIN BY
PAGE BROS (NORWICH) LTD

PREFACE

The year 1973 sees the introduction of two extensive reforms in the taxation arrangements of the United Kingdom. The unified system of personal taxation and the imputation system of corporation tax have been on the statute book for two years and one year respectively and it has been possible to foresee at least some of the problems which will arise. Already the Finance Act, 1973, has produced a rich crop of consequential amendments on matters overlooked in the earlier Acts. It has, among other things, applied the investment income surcharge to the whole of the income of discretionary trusts and accumulations of income, thus demonstrating that the old earned income relief is not quite dead.

A book on tax planning published so soon after such major changes must to some extent take the form of a simple text book on the new systems. Thus the chapters on companies have been considerably amended and rewritten with a view to giving a general explanation of advance corporation tax, tax credits and the new procedure of statutory apportionment which succeeds shortfall assessment. Share option schemes being once again allowed, albeit under strict control, we have added a chapter on them and share incentive schemes.

The Finance Act, 1972, dealt a lethal blow to those who had taken advantage of the earlier capital gains provisions relating to consideration payable by instalments, and various decisions in the courts have shown that complex schemes to avoid tax may get short shrift in the present climate of judicial opinion. This edition follows the policy of its predecessors in explaining how the taxpayer may regulate his affairs so as legitimately and openly to minimise the burden of taxation. It does not describe or recommend artificial schemes for tax avoidance. Where a path through the tax jungle exists the virtuous taxpayer may tread it, but he will hack a new way through the thickets at his peril.

We have followed the existing practical approach of the book and where appropriate have included summaries of points to which the busy practitioner may usefully refer when addressing himself to the problem of drafting a legitimate tax planning scheme for his clients. In the chapter on Partnerships we have added a section dealing with the vexed question of the purchase of goodwill. This is a problem which increasingly exercises professional men and women who traditionally carry on business in that way.

The book continues to embody the fruits of experience rather than abstract theory.

PHILIP LAWTON
ANTHONY SUMPTION

24 Old Buildings
Lincoln's Inn
London W.C.2.

Albion Chambers
Bristol

CONTENTS

TABLE OF CASES

TABLE OF STATUTES

Ah love!—Could thou and I with Fate conspire
To grasp this sorry Scheme of Things entire,
    Would we not shatter it to bits—and then
Remould it nearer to the Heart's Desire?

OMAR KHAYYAM

CHAPTER I

THE FAMILY UNIT

SINCE the purpose of personal tax planning is to conserve resources for the benefit of dependants, most of its operations take place within the family. It is important to start by considering how far the family forms a unit in tax law and how far its members can be treated as separate individuals.

So far as husband and wife are concerned, while living together they were up to 1972 almost completely one flesh for income tax and surtax. Previously there were only two exceptions to this rule, the first a procedural one allowing separate assessments to be claimed without reducing the total tax payable and the second a small relief confined to earned income.

From 6th April, 1972, s. 23 of the Finance Act, 1971, introduced the first real crack in the husband and wife unit. For 1972/73 and later years, there is a joint right to elect that the earnings of the wife should be taxed separately from the income of the husband, which still includes her unearned income, for all income tax purposes at all rates. Important though the departure is, its application to tax planning is limited, since any inflation of a wife's emoluments from a family company or business could result in the disallowance of the payments, in computing the payer's tax, on the ground that they were not wholly and exclusively incurred for the purposes of the trade or business. There are advantages if a wife becomes a partner in the family business, but she must not be a sleeping partner, because then her share of profits would not be earned income.

It will be seen in Chapters III to V that husband and wife are also identified under certain anti-avoidance provisions where a benefit to a spouse of the settlor produces the same result as a benefit to the settlor himself.

For estate duty, husband and wife have always been separate individuals so that if estate duty saving is the only concern a gift to a spouse is just as effective as a gift to anyone else, subject to any special rules applying to relatives (p. 10). There are two respects in which a spouse is treated differently from other relatives. The first is the exemption from duty on gifts to spouses up to £15,000 granted by s. 121 of the Finance Act, 1972. The other is the highly favourable exemption, under which settled property on which duty has been paid since the date of the settlement on the death of one spouse is not liable to duty again on the death of the survivor, if the survivor was not competent to deal with the capital. This is generally called "the surviving spouse exemption". As we shall see in Chapter II these two exemptions can lead to substantial reductions in liability to estate duty.

When one comes to capital gains tax, the position of husband and wife is even more favourable. Under para. 20 of Sched. 7 to the Finance Act, 1965, an outright disposal of assets other than trading stock between husband and wife living together is not chargeable to tax and the spouse acquiring the asset simply takes over the other's base value. But a gift in settlement is a chargeable disposal by virtue of s. 25 and although the spouse of the settlor may be the principal beneficiary, or even the sole beneficiary apart from the settlor himself, para. 20 does not apply.

The exemption from capital gains tax on death, introduced by s. 59 of the Finance Act, 1971, applies on the death of a surviving spouse entitled to a life interest, even though estate duty is not payable on the settled property because of the estate duty exemption. This is an exception to the general rule that exemption from capital gains tax on death is only given when there is a liability to estate duty on the same occasion.

Children are a different matter. For many years there have been anti-avoidance provisions, mentioned in Chapter IV, which tax as the income of the settlor any income paid to or applied for the benefit of a child of the settlor while he is an infant and unmarried. Until 5th April, 1972, the child was treated as an infant up to the age of twenty-one if not regularly working.

From 6th April, 1969, up to 5th April, 1972, investment income of an infant who was unmarried and not regularly working was treated as the income of the parent, whether it derived from the parent or not. This more general aggregation of infants' income was abolished for 1972/73 and later years by s. 16 of the Finance Act, 1971, and, at the same time, the age limit where the infant is a child of the settlor was reduced to eighteen in all cases.

These changes are an important reversal of the tendency towards a family unit. In particular the abolition of the general aggregation of an infant's investment income once again made it attractive to provide for grandchildren by covenants and settlements which skip a generation.

Under estate duty law children have never been in any special position. If they are affected by particular rules, it is simply because they fall within the category of relatives, although for the exemption of marriage gifts parents or ancestors of one of the parties have a £5,000 limit instead of the £1,000 limit applying to other people.

For capital gains tax, it has to be remembered that a gift to a child is a deemed disposal on which the donor will be liable to tax on any gain he is deemed to have realised.

CHAPTER II

BEQUESTS AND GIFTS INTER VIVOS

ESTATE DUTY

IN spite of the vulnerable period of seven years the simplest and most effective method of reducing estate duty is still an outright gift of property. This is even more the case following the passing of s. 121 of the Finance Act, 1972, which exempts from duty gifts, whether *inter vivos* or testamentary, to a surviving spouse up to a limit of £15,000. An even division of the family fortune between husband and wife is sound planning when the respective ages, the health of the partners and the health of the marriage are favourable.

If a man who originally had £60,000 dies more than seven years after giving his wife £30,000, having availed himself of the s. 121 exemption in his will, it will be found that the total duty on the two estates can have been reduced to about £1,250.

With the first £15,000 now duty free and the full amount of the exemption under s. 121 available, £30,000 of an estate escapes duty. If, in our example, the wife had no other means, her estate would, if she in her turn makes a will availing herself of s. 121, be duty free regardless of the seven-year period. However, were she to leave her estate outright to her husband, in the event of her dying before him, he would be faced with the problem of planning his estate anew. In such a case, therefore, the wife should leave her estate to him for life with the remainder over to other people, probably her children, thus escaping duty on his death under the surviving spouse exemption. So as not to impose hardship on the surviving spouse, power should be given to the executors to make advances of capital. Thus her estate of £30,000 should then be duty free not only on her death but also on the later death of her husband.

For the same reasons the husband should dispose of his

remaining £30,000 by a similar will so that in the event of his wife's death after him no duty would become due.

There are some limitations imposed by Sched. 26 to the Finance Act, 1972, on the type of gift exempted by the section. It does not apply if the gift depends upon a condition not satisfied within twelve months after death, or if it takes effect on the termination of any prior interest or of any period other than an interest or period terminating on or before the donor's death. However, the last limitation does not take effect where the gift is dependent on the widow or widower surviving the deceased spouse for a specified period.

Thus, after the seven-year period, by these judicious arrangements, much of our imaginary client's £60,000 would be duty free from one generation to the next.

If the donor dies within seven years of the gift it will be aggregated with his estate and for estate duty purposes this will be £60,000 again. £15,000 will be free of duty and £15,000 exempt from duty under s. 121, so the total duty will be £9,750.

Should the death of the donor occur after four years, s. 64 of the Finance Act, 1960, as amended by s. 35 of the Finance Act, 1968, provides what is informally called "taper relief" which reduces the value of the gift for estate duty purposes on the death of the donor:

If he survives the gift by 4 years, by 15 per cent.
If he survives the gift by 5 years, by 30 per cent.
If he survives the gift by 6 years, by 60 per cent.

If both spouses die within five years of each other the estate will qualify for quick succession relief under s. 30 of the Finance Act, 1958. This provides for the amount of duty to be reduced by a sliding scale percentage:

If the deaths occur within 3 months—75 per cent.
If the deaths occur within 1 year—50 per cent.
If the deaths occur within 2 years—40 per cent.
If the deaths occur within 3 years—30 per cent.
If the deaths occur within 4 years—20 per cent.
If the deaths occur within 5 years—10 per cent.

It will be seen that both forms of relief would be available in certain circumstances.

In the case of husband and wife, a settled gift has some advantages over an outright one when the donor's estate is too big to be absorbed by the exemption under s. 121. If the gift or part of it is settled on the donee for life so that she is not competent to dispose of the property, and the donor dies first, but towards the end of the seven-year period, the property will bear duty on the donor's death at the reduced value; the surviving spouse exemption nevertheless applies and no duty will be payable on the donee's death (Finance Act, 1894, s. 5 (2)). Settling the gift will also avoid the risk of double duty if the donee dies first and the donor follows within seven years of the gift; the property will pass and will bear duty on the death of the donee, but the surviving spouse exemption will apply on the death of the donor, since he was not competent to dispose of the property at any time during the continuance of the settlement.

Section 121 also exempts from duty gifts to charities up to £50,000 and gifts without limit to the bodies concerned with the national heritage which are referred to in Sched. 25 to the Act.

It is no longer necessary in the case of gifts under s. 121 to see that possession and enjoyment of the property comprised in the gift is assumed to the entire exclusion of the donor and of any benefit to him by contract or otherwise. "Gift" is defined for the purposes of the section by Sched. 26, para. 29, as any testamentary disposition and any disposition by virtue of which property passes on the death. Usually, reserving a benefit, such as a right to the income of the property, makes no difference in the case of husband and wife since their income is aggregated for tax purposes, but it is conceivable that in particular circumstances it might be worth while reserving some sort of benefit out of the property given.

It is still necessary to be certain that the gift is completed and where it is of greater value than £15,000 or where the donee is not a spouse, and the other exemptions are not involved, the old rule still applies and it is absolutely necessary that the donee should assume possession and enjoyment of the property to the entire exclusion of the donor and any benefit to him by contract or otherwise. Usually the donor is excluded at the time of the gift, but the leaving of this precaution to a later date does not matter, so long as it is effectively done outside the statutory period.

To understand how wide the latter condition is, it must be remembered that it consists of two legs; the donor has to be excluded from possession and enjoyment, as well as from any benefit by contract or otherwise. In view of the fact that the words "or otherwise" have to be construed *ejusdem generis* with "contract," some people think that a so-called gentlemen's agreement, by which income from the property is to be returned to the donor, does not prevent the gift escaping duty so long as the agreement is not legally enforceable. This may be true so far as the second leg is concerned, but if any part of the income or the property itself is actually returned to the donor, whether under an enforceable agreement or not, there is clearly a breach of the first leg. Even under the second leg, the force of the *ejusdem generis* rule has been weakened by s. 35 (3) of the Finance Act, 1959, by which a benefit obtained by associated operations is treated as a benefit by contract or otherwise.

On the other hand, a donor can make an effective gift of a particular interest in property, and the retention of a different interest in the same property does not matter. For example, in *Munro* v. *Stamp Duties Commissioner* [1934] A.C. 61, a sheep farmer gave to his children a reversionary interest in freehold land which was already let to a family partnership. The donor was one of the partners and as such he continued in joint occupation of the land until his death. The Privy Council held under a similar New South Wales statute that the gift was effective because the donor had been excluded from the thing actually given, namely the reversion. But in *Oakes* v. *Stamp Duties Commissioner* [1954] A.C. 57, remuneration payable to the settlor as trustee was held to be a benefit reserved out of the interests settled.

If a donor relying on the *Munro* case arranges for a lease to be granted to his nominee (since he cannot in law grant a lease to himself) before giving the land, he should not grant a lease for his life or determinable on his death, because this is expressly included in the definition of settlement by s. 36 (5) (*a*) (ii) of the

Finance Act, 1969, the reversion and not the lease being treated as the property attracting duty on his death.

The converse case arose in *Chick* v. *Stamp Duties Commissioner* [1958] A.C. 435, again in New South Wales, and led to legislation in this country. In that case, the donor gave business assets to his sons and *later* went into partnership with them. The Privy Council held that the donor had not been excluded from the assets, since he had subsequently acquired an interest in them under the partnership. The result of this hard decision was s. 35 of the Finance Act, 1959, which provides that certain events are to be disregarded if they take place for full consideration in money or money's worth. The section applies where the donor retains or assumes occupation of *land* which has been given, or enjoyment of an incorporeal right over it, and where he retains or assumes possession in the case of *chattels*. This would cover the facts in *Chick's* case, because the subsequent partnership was on a commercial basis, and it would also cover a case where the donor of a house later takes a lease of it at a rack-rent. In order to comply with the section it is essential that the rent shall be not less than the full market rent. Even if it was the intention of all parties that the proper sum should be paid, and owing to some mistake in assessing it, the District Valuer after the donor's death can show that it was inadequate, the whole benefit of s. 35 will be lost.

Section 35 does not throw any light on a common transaction, which caused some misgivings after the decision in *Chick's* case. This is the gift by husband to wife of the matrimonial home or furniture, when the husband continues to share it with the wife, as would normally be his expectation. Section 35 does not apply to these husband and wife gifts, because the husband does not usually give full consideration in money or money's worth for continuing to sleep in his bed or sit in his chair, but in spite of this the present practice of the Estate Duty Office is to concede that the husband has not retained an interest merely because his wife did not celebrate the gift by ejecting him.

In any case s. 121 now gives protection against duty to the extent of £15,000.

If there have been changes in the property between the date of the gift and the date of death, the question of whether the donor has been excluded at any particular time must be judged by reference to the property which would have been dutiable under the rules mentioned on p. 15, if the donor had died at that time.

Undivided Shares

When a person has placed property in the names of himself and another as beneficial joint tenants, there is strictly a claim for duty on the whole property on his death, however long after, under s. 38 (2) (*b*) of the Customs and Inland Revenue Act, 1881, incorporated in s. 2 (1) (*c*) of the Finance Act, 1894. By a concession, not limited to husband and wife, the share of the donee is charged on the more lenient basis of a gift. This means that the donee's share escapes duty if the donor survives the transaction by seven years, and the sliding scale applies if he dies in the fifth, sixth or seventh year, provided that the donor was excluded from possession and enjoyment and from any benefit by contract or otherwise. For this purpose residence in the property by the donor is not treated as non-exclusion.

If the property placed in joint names consists of investments it is essential that a half share of the income should be separately received by the donee, and not paid into an account on which the donor has power to draw.

The severable share which the donor continues to hold is dutiable on his death, as property of which he was competent to dispose, and in the case of husband and wife is entitled to the benefit of the s. 121 exemption.

In the case of tenants in common, the same estate duty position can be achieved, but without relying on the concession. Sometimes the matrimonial home is vested in the husband and wife as beneficial tenants in common, rather than as joint tenants, with a view to each settling his or her share on the other for life, either *inter vivos* or by will, in order to obtain the benefit of the surviving spouse exemption on the second death. The advantages, as between husband and wife, of a settlement with reverter to disponer are mentioned in Chapter VI.

Sales to Relatives

A sale is not a gift, and before 1950 it could not be treated as one merely because the vendor made a bad bargain, whether the sale was between relatives or strangers. It was necessary for the Inland Revenue to go further and prove that a sale at an undervalue contained an "element of bounty" (*Re Earl Fitzwilliam's Agreement* [1950] Ch. 448), in which case duty might be charged on the value of the property, the value of the consideration being deducted by concession. Section 44 of the Finance Act, 1940, as amended by s. 46 of the Finance Act, 1950, altered the law in the case of sales to relatives, and this is of great importance since most tax planning transactions take place within the family. "Relative," in this context, means a spouse, parent, child, uncle or aunt of the deceased, the issue of any of these people and the spouse of any such person or issue, illegitimate and adopted children being included. The effect of the section is to reverse the onus of proof, and sales to relatives are treated as gifts, unless it can be shown that full consideration in money or money's worth was given to the deceased for his own use or benefit. If the donee provided the donor with an annuity for the life of the donor or of anyone else, this does not count as consideration, although a deduction from the estate duty valuation of the property is given for the total of annuity payments actually made before the death so far as this exceeds a reasonable return from the property. When the section applies, duty is charged on the value of the property at the appropriate date for valuation (see p. 15) after making a deduction for the consideration actually given, in the same proportion as the consideration bore to the value of the property at the date of the gift.

The rules about dispositions to relatives cannot be avoided by the intervention of a controlled company. They apply if the deceased made a disposition to the company and a relative of his was a member of the company at the date of the disposition or at any subsequent time before the death. If on the other hand a company controlled by the deceased made a gift to the relative, it is possible to look through the company by the statutory device of treating the company as a trustee for its members, debenture holders and loan creditors, in order to see whether there was really a gift by the deceased. The same device is used for the purpose of deciding whether, and to what extent, the deceased really received consideration in money or money's worth.

These provisions make it essential that evidence of value should be preserved whenever there is a sale by one member of the family to another.

Exemptions

In addition to s. 121 of the Finance Act, 1972, there are certain other cases in which a gift may operate immediately to save duty without the donor surviving for any particular period:

(1) *Normal expenditure.*—By s. 37 of the Finance Act, 1968, a gift made after 19th March, 1968, is exempt from estate duty if the Board of Inland Revenue, or the court on appeal, is satisfied about three things:

(*a*) that the gift was part of the normal expenditure of the deceased;

(*b*) that it was made out of his income; and

(*c*) that allowing for all such gifts the deceased was left with sufficient income to maintain his usual standard of living.

Gifts made on or before 19th March, 1968, can qualify for exemption under the slightly wider wording of s. 59 (2) of the Finance (1909–10) Act, 1910, where the deceased's income is only one of the factors in deciding whether the expenditure was reasonable as well as normal. On the other hand, the right of appeal to the court does not apply, the exemption under the older section being entirely at the discretion of the Board.

It is not always realised how extensive the exemption is, even under the definition in s. 37; quite a small element of regularity may enable the benefit of it to be obtained. The greater the donor's income, the easier it is to show that gifts fulfil the conditions and it is precisely in those cases where the rate of duty will be high that the exemption is most likely to be available. It is the practice to treat the capital element of a purchased life annuity as income for this purpose, even though it is exempted from tax by s. 230.

Under s. 34 of the Finance Act, 1959, premiums paid by

the deceased to keep up a policy on his life for the benefit of a donee are treated as gifts of rights under the policy. Now that non-aggregation of policy moneys has been abolished in the case of gifts, the normal expenditure exemption provides the principal means of escaping estate duty on life policies, since the proceeds of a policy to which s. 34 applies will not be liable to duty if the premiums were normal expenditure of the deceased. This is particularly important in connection with the payment of premiums by a wife out of her income, since the burden of maintaining her standard of living falls generally on the husband, leaving the wife a larger margin for normal expenditure. Section 37 (2) of the Finance Act, 1968, imposes one restriction; a premium paid under a combined life assurance and annuity scheme (see pp. 147–148) cannot be counted as normal expenditure and the same applies to a gift used directly to pay such a premium.

(2) *Marriage gifts.*—Gifts made after 19th March, 1968, are exempt only within the limits set by s. 36 of the Finance Act, 1968. The section divides gifts in consideration of marriage into two classes:

(*a*) Gifts, whether outright or settled, made by one of the parties to the marriage or a parent or ancestor of one of the parties. Here the exemption applies to a gift up to a value of £5,000 or to the first £5,000 of a larger gift;

(*b*) Gifts made by donors not so closely connected with the marriage, where the exemption applies only to a gift up to a value of £1,000 or to the first £1,000 of a larger gift.

These limits apply to any one death in respect of any one marriage. This means that a man who has given £5,000 to each of his children on marriage and £1,000 to each of his nephews and nieces on marriage can look forward to all the gifts being exempt on his death. Correspondingly, one marriage might attract a total exemption of, say, £22,000 if the two parents of the bride, the two parents of the bridegroom and a couple of uncles all gave the maximum amounts. If the limit has to be applied to more than one gift, for example, if a father settled £20,000 for his daughter on marriage and also gave her £10,000 outright, the relief is split between the gifts rateably according to their values. In all cases the values referred to are the values of the gifts before applying the sliding scale under s. 64 of the Finance Act, 1960.

The 1968 Act limited the exemption for gifts after 19th March, 1968, but did not alter the existing law about the meaning of a gift in consideration of marriage.

The gift must be made before the marriage or in pursuance of an agreement made before the marriage. With a formal marriage settlement, there is no difficulty in proving the connection between the gift and the marriage. In the case of an outright gift, the counsel of perfection would be to have a written agreement under which the gift became unconditional when the marriage took place. The Estate Duty Office does not insist on this and it is sufficient if there is evidence that the marriage was the consideration for the gift. Nor does the gift have to be made within any particular period before the marriage, provided that it is not made until the marriage has been arranged; if the donor were to die after making the gift but before the marriage, the exemption would still apply, assuming that the marriage did in fact take place.

In *Rennell* v. *Commissioners of Inland Revenue* [1964] A.C. 173, the House of Lords held that a settlement might be made in consideration of marriage even though the benefits were not confined to persons within the marriage consideration. This decision led to the passing of s. 53 of the Finance Act, 1963, which defines the cases where a gift *inter vivos* can be treated as one made in consideration of marriage. If it is an outright gift, it must not be made to anyone except a party to the marriage. If it is a gift in settlement, the beneficial interests must be confined to people described in the section, who are roughly speaking the classes of beneficiary one would expect to find in the traditional marriage settlement; reasonable remuneration for the trustees can be provided.

As a result of the decision in the Chancery Division in *Commissioners of Inland Revenue* v. *Park* [1971] 2 All E.R. 161, it was thought that it might not be sufficient that a marriage was the occasion of the gift if surrounding circumstances showed it was not the real consideration. This decision has been reversed by the Court of Appeal ([1972] 1 All E.R. 394) which held *inter alia* that the purpose or motive of the settlor was irrelevant where the settlement was expressed to be made in consideration of marriage and the sole absolute beneficiary under the settlement was a spouse of the marriage in question.

Section 64 of the Finance Act, 1963, puts the exemption from stamp duty for gifts in consideration of marriage on exactly the same basis as the estate duty exemption under s. 53. This has not been affected by the 1968 Act, so that stamp duty exemption can still be claimed for gifts outside the limits of £5,000 or £1,000.

There is no relief from capital gains tax for marriage gifts.

(3) *Small gifts.*—The Finance (1909–10) Act, 1910, exempted gifts not exceeding in total £100 in the case of any one donee. A more important exemption is contained in the Finance Act, 1949, s. 33, under which gifts not exceeding in total £500 in the case of any one donee are exempted, provided that the gift did not include any interest in settled property and that bona fide possession and enjoyment were immediately assumed by the donee and retained to the exclusion of the donor. The two exemptions cannot both be claimed at once and the first is therefore no longer of any value, except in cases where the conditions of the second are not satisfied. In order to see whether the limits apply, the whole of the gifts to a particular donee have to be taken into account, except those which would not in any event be dutiable because they were made outside the statutory period, or in consideration of marriage, or as part of the normal expenditure of the deceased. In the case of the £500 exemption, marginal relief has been given by s. 38 (11) of the Finance Act, 1957; the duty is limited to the

excess of the gifts over £500, so that the donee can no longer be left with less than he would have had if the gifts had amounted to £500 and no more.

Valuation

Since the ordinary principles of valuation for estate duty apply to gifts, it is generally necessary to ascertain the open market value of the property given as at the date of the donor's death. In the case of shares in a family company, the assets basis of valuation discussed in Chapter VIII may apply instead of the open market basis. The difficulties begin when it has to be decided what property is to be valued, and these difficulties arise in two ways.

(*a*) *Changes in the property*

Much may happen in seven years, and before the donor dies the property may have been sold, given away or settled, or (in the case of a racehorse) have predeceased the donor. The law on this question is contained in s. 38 of the Finance Act, 1957, one of the longest and most difficult to follow of the estate duty sections. Briefly, the position is that gifts of money are gifts of money and do not change, settled gifts have to be valued according to what is in the settlement at the date of death but excluding accumulated interest, while gifts which are neither monetary nor settled are dealt with as follows:

> If the donee disposes of the property given, for full consideration, the proceeds of sale or the property he receives in exchange are substituted for the original subject-matter of the gift.
>
> If the donee voluntarily disposes of the property without receiving full consideration, the original property continues to be the subject of the charge to duty, but its value at the donor's death is taken to be the value at the date of disposition. This means that, if the original property were one attracting a reduced rate of duty, such as agricultural property, the relief could still be claimed.
>
> If the donee settles the property the gift has to be valued according to what is in the settlement at the date of the

donor's death, just as if he had himself made a settled gift. Apparently this applies even to a gift of money, although in practice it might be difficult to identify a money gift with a settlement subsequently made by the donee.

The result of these rules is that the true deceased racehorse still escapes duty, but most of the imitation ones are non-starters. It will be seen from this that in inflationary times such as the present, where the value of money falls and that of assets, particularly land, often increases, it is wise to give cash, even if this is then used to buy the assets which the donor really wishes to give. If this is done, attention must be paid to the effect of s.44 of the Finance Act, 1940, discussed on p. 10, *supra*.

When the donee of shares becomes entitled to a bonus issue or rights issue before the donor's death, the new shares are included in the gift, subject to a deduction for any payment made in the case of a rights issue.

(*b*) *Gifts not the same at both ends*

Whenever there is a difference between what the donor gives and what the donee receives, the valuation for estate duty will depend on whether one looks a gift horse in the mouth or the tail. In *Potter* v. *Lord Advocate* [1958] S.C. 213 where a father gave his son a cheque in favour of a company to enable the son to subscribe for shares, the Scottish court decided it was the sum of money which was given, not the shares. Some doubt was thrown on the decision in *Potter's* case by *Ralli Bros. Trustee Co., Ltd.* v. *Commissioners of Inland Revenue* [1968] Ch. 215, in which it was held that the payment by a settlor of the first premium for a policy in the name of the trustees was a gift of the policy rather than the money. It would be wise for anyone wanting to make a gift of money to give the donee a cheque in his own favour and let the donee deal with the application of the money himself.

If money is given to enable the donee to complete a purchase of land, it is advisable that the donee, and not the donor, should be the person to enter into the contract in the first place, because if the donor has already entered into the contract himself, it is difficult to arrange the completion in such a way that the subject matter of the gift is cash rather than the property.

INCOME TAX

An outright gift of capital is always effective to transfer the future income from the donor to the donee for tax purposes, except in two cases:

(1) If the donee is the wife of the donor there will usually be no tax saving for the simple reason that the income of a married woman living with her husband is deemed to be his (s. 37). Unearned income of the wife is not affected by s. 23 of the Finance Act, 1971 (see Chapter I), but in a proper case a gift of a partnership share might produce earned income on which the wife could be separately taxed.

(2) It was held in *Thomas* v. *Marshall* [1953] A.C. 543, that an outright gift to an infant child of the settlor is within the definition of settlement in s. 444, and accordingly the income from the property given is treated as that of the settlor so long as the donee remains an infant and unmarried (see Chapter IV).

In the case of settled gifts there are a number of fences to be jumped before the settlement is effective to deprive the settlor of his income; these are contained in ss. 437–459, mentioned in Chapters III and IV.

CAPITAL GAINS TAX

Under s. 22 (4) of the Finance Act, 1965, a gift is deemed to be a disposal at the market value of the asset except where the gift is to charity or one of the *national heritage bodies;* on any gain he is assumed to have made, the donor is liable to tax at 30 per cent., unless a lower rate is produced under s. 21 by treating one half of the chargeable gain up to £5,000, plus the whole of the excess, as income liable to income tax at all rates. If the donor makes default in paying the tax for twelve months, the donee can be called on to pay it with a right, if he is more successful than the Revenue were, to recover it from the donor.

This liability to capital gains tax is not a fatal objection to the giving of assets, but does call for some care in selection. For example it will often be wise to choose assets which have not yet substantially appreciated, particularly if they are likely to begin appreciating in the future. At the same time it should be remembered that the gain on any asset retained by the donor will be wiped out on his death. If estate duty is payable because the donor dies within seven years after the gift, then para. 14 of Sched. 12 to the Finance Act, 1971, gives the donee a new base value at the date of the death for the purpose of future capital gains tax, but without any charge on the gain accrued up to the death; this only wipes out the gain between the date of the gift and the death of the donor. A donor cannot generally build up a useful loss by giving an asset which has depreciated; apart from certain gifts in settlement for educational, cultural or recreational purposes (para. 12 of Sched. 19 to the Finance Act, 1969), a loss on a disposal to a connected person can only be set against a chargeable gain on some other disposal to the same person (para. 17 (3) of Sched. 7 to the 1965 Act). If the assets given consist of land, unquoted shares or business assets, s. 117 of the Finance Act, 1972, allows the tax to be paid by eight equal yearly instalments or sixteen half-yearly instalments, with interest, the first instalment being due twelve months after the date of the disposal. The privilege cannot be used to defer the payment of tax on a disguised gift of cash in circumstances where it has to be raised by the sale of assets, because if the assets are disposed of for valuable consideration by the donee, or any subsequent owner, the balance of the tax on the original gift becomes payable forthwith.

Gifts are included in the disposals to which the following capital gains tax exemptions apply:

(1) Private motor cars.

(2) Assets with a market value not exceeding £100 in any one year of assessment (this exemption is confined to gifts).

(3) Saving certificates.

(4) Life policies unless disposed of by a purchaser.

(5) Equitable interests under settlements, unless disposed of by a purchaser.

(6) Private residences.

(7) Tangible moveables with a value not exceeding

£1,000 for each article or set of articles, marginal relief being given for values slightly over £1,000.

(8) Retirement relief on transfer of business assets (see p. 46).

(9) Gilt-edged securities, unless disposed of within twelve months after acquisition.

(10) Total disposals in a year of assessment not exceeding £500 in amount or value, with marginal relief. There is also a special treatment, under s. 119 of the Finance Act, 1972, of gifts and other disposals not at arm's length, without limit of amount, to a charity or one of the bodies concerned with the national heritage. In the case of a gift, the disposal is treated as giving rise to neither a gain nor a loss.

It is also worth pointing out that a chargeable gain can arise only on the gift of an asset, as distinct from a gift of cash. This adds force to the suggestion on p. 16, that gifts should so far as possible always be in cash, except perhaps where advantage can be taken of s. 117 of the Finance Act, 1972, which allows payment of capital gains tax on disposal of certain assets to be made by instalments, or of s. 119 relating to gifts to charity or the national heritage bodies.

Except for disposals of trading stock, a gift between husband and wife living together can be made without any capital gains tax consequences, as a result of the joint effect of para. 30 of Sched. 6 and para. 20 of Sched. 7 to the Finance Act, 1965. If the asset was one already held by the donor on 6th April, 1965, the other spouse takes over any right to elect, on a future disposal, for market value at that date to be taken as the base.

SUMMARY OF PRACTICAL POINTS

(1) Where the estate is likely to exceed £15,000 but be less than £30,000 a gift of the excess to the spouse, either *inter vivos* or by will, should suffice.

(2) If the estate of the surviving spouse is likely, with the gift, to exceed £15,000, or where the donor wishes to "tie it up," the gift can be settled either by deed or will so as to take advantage of

the surviving spouse exemption. Power for the trustees to make advances of capital is often advisable.

(3) When the estate exceeds £30,000 a straightforward division by gift *inter vivos* is usually the most effective planning. It should be accompanied by mutual wills by spouses in favour of each other to take advantage again of the s. 121 exemption after the seven year period or the appropriate period for the "taper relief" has expired.

(4) Those with large disposable incomes should consider adopting a settled practice of making gifts which can qualify for exemption under s. 37 of the Finance Act, 1968, as normal expenditure.

(5) Gifts on marriage should always be considered when opportunity arises. The donor need not be related to the parties to the marriage, but if they are not children or remoter issue only £1,000 escapes duty.

(6) When considering gifts of assets which may increase in value it is wise to see if the gift can initially be made in the form of cash which can be used to buy the asset. If this course is adopted evidence of value should be preserved.

CHAPTER III

SETTLEMENTS IN GENERAL

SETTLEMENTS are an ancient tax planning device, having been employed for centuries before income tax and estate duty for the avoidance of fiscal burdens and legal restrictions put upon citizens by governments. Today, as in former times, it is probably only those with larger estates and incomes who will find it worth while to consider making settlements, and these have been attacked by successive Finance Acts over many years so that the Income and Corporation Taxes Act contains nineteen sections dealing specifically with settlements or settlors.

For income tax purposes the standard device of the Acts is to deem income of the settlement to be that of the settlor, while for estate duty purposes it is to make the capital pass at death, although in actual fact it has passed in the deceased's lifetime.

If, therefore, any settlement is to be effective in saving tax it must comply with the stringent conditions laid down in the Act, some of which apply to all settlements, and some only to certain classes such as discretionary trusts and those in favour of infants. This chapter deals with the provisions of the Act which apply to all settlements, and in the following two chapters we shall deal with the other types.

A settlement is defined for income tax purposes by s. 454 (3) as "any disposition, trust, covenant, agreement or arrangement." Section 444 (2) adds "transfer of assets" to this list for the purpose of children's settlements. "Settlor" is defined as including any person by whom the settlement was made and a person is deemed to have made a settlement if he has made or entered into it directly or indirectly and in particular any person who has provided or undertaken to provide funds directly or indirectly for the purpose of the settlement, or has made with any other person a reciprocal arrangement for that other person to make or enter into the settlement.

These definitions are very wide and bring within the restrictions laid down in the Act most, if not all, possible forms of settlement whatever they may be called and however indirect their effect.

A settlor cannot escape the operation of the sections by leaving his affairs in the hands of professional advisers and allowing them to work out a scheme of which the details are unknown to him, since this would be an arrangement (*Crossland* v. *Hawkins* [1961] Ch. 537).

By s. 446, the whole income of a revocable settlement is deemed to be the income of the settlor; a settlement is revocable if any person has the power, whether immediately or in the future, to revoke or otherwise determine the settlement or any provision of the settlement, or to diminish the property comprised in it, to the benefit of the settlor or the wife or husband of the settlor. In the case of a power which cannot be exercised within the period of six years from the time when any particular property first became comprised in the settlement, the section does not apply so long as the power is not exercisable.

By s. 447, if the settlor has an interest in any income arising under the settlement, or in any property comprised in it, then so long as this state of affairs continues any undistributed income of the settlement, which generally means income accumulated by the trustees, is deemed to be the income of the settlor. There is no six-year breathing space in this section, because it is aimed at income which is not transferred to someone else but is actually being piled up for the settlor to resume at a later date and to wait six years would be far too small a price for such a privilege.

The settlor has an interest for this purpose if any income or property which may at any time arise under or be comprised in the settlement is, or will or may become, payable to or applicable for the benefit of the settlor or the wife or husband of the settlor in any circumstances whatsoever. It will be noticed that a mere possibility of benefit is sufficient to bring the section into operation, but at least there is authority for saying that the only matters to be taken into account are those arising either under the trusts of the settlement or under some collateral arrangement having legal force (*Muir* v. *Commissioners of Inland Revenue* (1966), 43 T.C., at p. 381).

Usually a benefit by contract or otherwise which renders a gift ineffective for estate duty saving will also amount to an interest of the settlor under s. 447, but there are certain differences between the two provisions. It appears from *dicta* of the House of Lords in *Vestey's Executors* v. *Commissioners of Inland Revenue* (1949), 31 T.C. 1, that transactions on commercial terms between the settlor and the trustees, even if the settlor derives an "incidental benefit", are not caught by the section, which suggests that the remuneration for management services held in *Oakes* (p. 7) to be fatal for estate duty would not be a benefit within the meaning of s. 447. It was also said in the *Vestey* case that "payable to or applicable for the benefit of" should be read as a whole, so that the Revenue cannot pick on the word "payable" and ignore the element of benefit.

On the other hand benefits, or possible benefits, to a spouse of the settlor are within s. 447, but would be irrelevant for estate duty where husband and wife are treated as separate people.

The earlier decisions on s. 447 were considered by Goff, J., in *Commissioners of Inland Revenue* v. *Wachtel* [1947] 1 All E.R. 271. In that case the settlor deposited money interest free with a bank which lent the same amount to the trustees of the settlement at 1 per cent interest. It was part of the arrangement that the trustees should repay the bank out of accumulated income of the settlement and on each repayment made by the trustees the settlor was entitled to reduce his deposit to the same extent. It was held that the payments of the settlement income to the bank were for the benefit of the settlor, since they entitled him to withdraw an equivalent amount of frozen capital. The accumulated income of the settlement was accordingly taxable on the settlor.

A settlor is not deemed to have an interest in the income merely because it may revert to him on the happening of certain specified events, of which the most important is the death under the age of twenty-five or some lower age of some person who would be beneficially entitled to the income or property on attaining that age. It is for this reason that the vesting of shares under a settlement in children or issue should not be postponed beyond the age of twenty-five if there is any possibility of the funds reverting to the settlor.

Income arising under the settlement, whether distributed or not, is treated by s. 448 as the income of the settlor if there is power, under the terms of the settlement, to benefit the settlor or the wife or husband of the settlor. Since the section is confined to discretionary trusts, it is dealt with in Chapter V.

A most formidable section which the tax planner must consider very carefully when drafting a settlement is s. 451. Its ramifications are not as familiar as they might be—except to the Revenue officials responsible for investigating settlements. It would be well for settlors and their advisers to be equally knowledgeable, because as Russell, L. J., pointed out in *Commissioners of Inland Revenue* v. *De Vigier* (1963), 42 T.C. 24, "The pit dug by the Legislature is, perhaps inevitably, wide enough to catch the unwary innocent". The Revenue have been showing an increasing interest in applying s. 451 and their interest is not confined to cases of deliberate tax avoidance.

The section catches capital sums paid directly or indirectly to a settlor or his wife by the trustees of a settlement, to the extent of the net income accumulated under the settlement in the year of payment and in any previous year. Where it applies the effect is drastic, because the capital sum has to be grossed up and the whole amount is liable to tax as income of the settlor in the year of payment. If the capital sum is greater than the net accumulations of income up to date, the balance can be carried forward indefinitely, which means in effect that any accumulations in future years are treated as the settlor's income of those years until the capital sum is wiped out.

The aim of the section is clear: to prevent a settlor putting his money into an accumulating settlement for the benefit of his dependants, so that the income can be added free of higher rate tax at one end, while the trustees return to him an equivalent amount from the other end in the form of non-taxable capital advances.

While the object of s. 451 is a perfectly legitimate one, the troubles of the unwary begin with the wide definition of *capital sum,* which means:

"(i) any sum paid by way of loan or repayment of a loan; and

(ii) any other sum paid otherwise than as income, being a sum which is not paid for full consideration in money or money's worth".

The important thing to notice here is that a loan or repayment of a loan, in contrast to, say, a genuine purchase from the settlor, is not excluded from the definition by the presence of full consideration, and it does not matter how short lived the loan may be. In *Inland Revenue Commissioners* v. *De Vigier, supra,* the settlor had made a settlement for the benefit of his infant children and income was being accumulated free of surtax, as permitted by s. 438 (2) (*a*) (see p. 30). In 1957 the trustees, needing liquid funds to obtain a desirable investment, borrowed £7,000 from the settlor's wife, who was herself one of the trustees, and repaid it in 1958. The settlor was assessed to surtax for 1958–59 on the £7,000 (grossed-up) under the provisions re-enacted in s. 451.

The settlor's only defence was a technical argument, taken from the law of trusts, that the transaction did not amount to a contract of loan by the wife, because she had merely relied on the equitable rights of a trustee who mixes his own money with the trust fund. The House of Lords unanimously held that this was not the correct inference from the facts proved, and that the settlor's wife had received a sum by way of repayment of loan within the meaning of the section.

Before *De Vigier,* these provisions had been considered in *Potts' Executors* v. *Commissioners of Inland Revenue* [1951] A.C. 443, where the decision of the House of Lords showed that, although the section bears harshly on loans, there are other transactions that escape it with surprising ease. The House decided that a payment to a third party in discharge of a debt owing by the settlor to the third party was not a sum paid to the settlor, either directly or indirectly; these words mean a payment into the settlor's hands or to someone accountable to him. Thus a payment to the settlor for the purpose of enabling him to discharge a debt to his bank was caught by the section in

Commissioners of Inland Revenue v. *Bates* (1966), 44 T.C. 225, another House of Lords decision which should be studied on the question of how the income is assessed. In *Commissioners of Inland Revenue* v. *Wachtel,* already mentioned in connection with s. 447, an alternative claim under s. 451 failed on the ground that the repayments by the trustees were made to the bank and not to the settlor.

Another real trap is subs. (4) of s. 451, which mentions with disarming brevity that a capital sum paid to the settlor (including his wife) by a body corporate connected with the settlement shall be treated as having been paid by the trustees. A body corporate is connected with the settlement in any year of assessment if it is at any time in the year a close company (or one that would be a close company if it were resident in the United Kingdom) of which the trustees or a beneficiary are participators.

Now this sort of connection between a company and a settlement is extremely common and arises whenever the shares of a family company are settled; both in *Potts'* case and *Bates'* case the payments had actually been made by a connected company and not by the trustees. The result is that all transactions between the settlor or his wife and the family company must be carefully watched, if there is to be a successful accumulation under the settlement, and in particular any sort of running account with the company must be avoided.

Another pitfall must be avoided when the settlement is first created. The section attacks any capital sum paid in any year of assessment by a company connected with the settlement in that year. If a company pays a capital sum to a settlor (perhaps by repaying a loan) in order to put its house in order before the settlement is created it will be caught if the settlement comes into existence and the company becomes connected with it subsequently but in the same year of assessment. As Polonius advised, "Neither a borrower nor a lender be".

Section 457, which applies only for the additional and higher rates of tax, is more familiar in connection with deeds of covenant but it may also cause the income from a capital settlement to be treated as income of the settlor, if the settlor has not divested himself absolutely of the property. This is shown by the decision in

Vandervell v. *Commissioners of Inland Revenue* [1967] 2 A.C. 291, where the settlor was assessed to surtax on the income arising under a charitable settlement because there was a possibility that upon the exercise of a certain option the capital would have been applicable for his benefit. For this purpose, the settlor has not divested himself absolutely if the property or income is, or will or may become, payable to or applicable for the benefit of the settlor or the wife or husband of the settlor in any circumstances whatsoever. Section 457 is further discussed in Chapter VII in relation to deeds of covenant.

It will have been noticed that there is considerable overlap between some of these sections. The same transaction may result in the settlor having retained an interest under s. 447, having received a capital sum under s. 451 and having failed to divest himself absolutely under s. 457. On the other hand a payment which escapes one section may be caught by another, as happened in *Commissioners of Inland Revenue* v. *Wachtel*.

The Settlor as Trustee

It is a natural reaction for a settlor to want to act as trustee of his own settlement. In deciding whether he should be allowed to do so, the following points ought to be considered:

(1) If a settlor-trustee concurs in an advance to a relative under the terms of the settlement, this could be treated as a disposition under s. 44 (1) of the Finance Act, 1940 (as amended by s. 46 of the 1950 Act), giving rise to a claim for duty on the settlor's death within seven years after the advance. The Estate Duty Office do not in practice take this point if the settlement was created outside the period and is otherwise unobjectionable.

(2) If the settlement includes shares of a family company, the settlor should not be first-named trustee, because then the settled shares would still count towards control for the purposes of s. 55 of the Finance Act, 1940 (see p. 79). It is safer that he should not be a trustee at all.

(3) Again in the case of shares of a family company, if the settlor is a director, pension schemes may be affected by registration of shares in his name (see p. 77).

(4) If the settlor is a trustee, care must be taken that he cannot benefit under a charging clause.

(5) After the creation of the settlement, the trustees may wish to buy assets from the settlor. There is no tax objection to trustees buying assets from the settlor at market value, but there might be difficulties under the law of trusts if the settlor were a trustee himself.

(6) From a practical point of view, a settlor who is at all unbusinesslike should be encouraged not to act as trustee in case he gets the trust money mixed with his own.

Practical Points in connection with Settlements Generally

(1) Make sure that the settlement is irrevocable within the extended definition contained in ss. 439, 445 and 446.

(2) See that the settlor and his wife (but not necessarily his widow) are excluded from any benefit in any circumstances whatsoever. The safest way is to include in the settlement an overriding clause to this effect.

(3) If shares in a family company are being settled, consider the loan position between the settlor and the company. If repayments have to be made by the company they should be made in a year of assessment before that in which the settlement is made or to a third person. But be careful that the latter is not merely the agent of the settlor.

(4) During the existence of a trust the settlor should be careful never to borrow from the company. The smallest shareholding will bring the company within s. 451 and make it a body corporate connected with the settlement.

(5) Avoid if possible having the settlor as trustee for the reasons set out above.

CHAPTER IV

INFANT SETTLEMENTS

ESTATE DUTY

THE simplest form of family settlement is a trust for the benefit of an infant contingently on his attaining the age of eighteen or some greater age. From the point of view of estate duty on the death of the settlor, any settlement should be looked on as merely a species of gift to which the rules in Chapter II may apply. Indeed, if the intended donee is an infant, the infant settlement may be the natural way of making the gift, because an outright transfer is impracticable.

If the settlement provides for the property to revert to the settlor on the death of the beneficiary under a certain age, this will not amount to a reservation out of the subject matter of the gift so as to prevent the seven-year rule applying (*New South Wales Stamp Duties Commissioner* v. *Perpetual Trust Co.* [1943] A.C. 425). On the death of the settlor outside the seven-year period, duty could only be charged on the value of the reversion itself, which would usually be negligible.

The fact that the trustees have a discretion to maintain the beneficiary, while he is under full age, does not make the settlement a discretionary settlement for the purposes of estate duty under s. 2 (1) (*b*) of the Finance Act, 1894 (see p. 39). The Estate Duty Office treat the word "maintenance" in this context as having the same meaning as the phrase "maintenance, education and benefit" in s. 31 of the Trustee Act, 1925, with the result that the exercise of the statutory power, or a similar express power, does not of itself give rise to a charge to estate duty on the settled property if the infant dies before becoming entitled.

INCOME TAX

One of the advantages of an infant settlement used to be the right to reclaim income tax in respect of income accumulated for the benefit of a person contingently on attaining a specified age or marrying. Within six years after the happening of the contingency, the beneficiary could claim the repayments to which his personal allowances would have entitled him throughout the whole period, if the income had been his, but this right to reclaim tax no longer applies to income for years of assessment after 1968–69. The right will still be available for the earlier years and the need to make the claim will arise for a long time to come as beneficiaries become entitled.

On the other hand, there are considerable tax advantages of accumulating income under an infant settlement, so long as various statutory conditions are observed.

Because of the legislation now contained in ss. 437–444, it is not possible for income which formerly belonged to a settlor to be spent on his own infant child without that income being treated for tax purposes as if it were still the income of the settlor. By s. 437, any income under a settlement to which the section applies, paid to or for the benefit of a child of the settlor in any year of assessment, is treated for all the purposes of the Act as the income of the settlor for that year if at the time of the payment the child was unmarried and was under eighteen. Section 438 (1) takes the matter further by providing that, if the income is so dealt with under the settlement that the income or assets representing it may benefit a child of the settlor in any circumstances in the future, the income is deemed to be paid to or for the benefit of that child. If matters stopped there, income accumulated for an infant child would be caught, but s. 438 (2) goes on to exempt from subs. (1) income accumulated under an irrevocable settlement of capital. Section 439 defines the meaning of "irrevocable", the most important point being that a settlement is not deemed to be revocable by reason only that it contains provisions for the determination of the settlement, so long as the settlor or the wife or husband of the settlor cannot benefit from the determination of the settlement during the lifetime of the child.

We have seen in the case of *Crossland* v. *Hawkins* (p. 22) that a settlor cannot escape the operation of the sections by leaving others to set up the trust and work out the details of the scheme. That was a case in which a distinguished actor arranged to work for a company so that it would get his fees, and as the company was owned by a settlement made by his father-in-law, of which his children were beneficiaries, they would eventually receive this income. It was held that this was an arrangement and Mr. Hawkins was the settlor. An almost exactly similar scheme was set up for a child actress, Miss Hayley Mills, and it was decided in the Court of Appeal (*Mills* v. *Inland Revenue Commissioners* [1972] 3 All E.R. 977) that because Miss Mills was a child who did not understand what was being done in her name *Crossland* v. *Hawkins* could be distinguished and Miss Mills could not be the settlor. It seems likely, therefore, that s. 444 in this sort of case will be considered by the House of Lords, and it is possible that in the case of children who are entitled to income of their own, apart from any settlement, a very narrow loophole may be open.

If the settlor has reserved a reversion in the settled property in the event of the death of the beneficiary under a particular age, it is essential that this age should not be greater than twenty-five, otherwise the income will be deemed to be that of the settlor under s. 447 (2) or 457 (6).

Form of Settlement

It follows from ss. 437–444 that a settlement for the benefit of an infant child of the settlor can only be effective for saving the higher rates of tax if it is an irrevocable settlement of capital and the income is accumulated for the benefit of the infant. If this type of settlement is used, and the other statutory requirements described in the previous chapter are observed, there is the great advantage that accumulated income escapes all liability to the higher rates of tax. This is because the higher rates are a tax on individuals and, so long as income is being validly accumulated for a beneficiary who is only contingently entitled, there is no individual who can be assessed to the tax. It was held by the Privy Council in *Houry* v. *Commissioner of Income Tax* [1960] A.C. 36, on similar provisions of the East African tax laws, that when trustees for an infant child of the settlor held shares in a controlled company on which a surtax direction was made the income notionally apportioned to the trustees was not deemed to be that of the settlor. In other words, the Inland Revenue cannot rely on a double deeming to bring home to the settlor income which has never in fact been distributed by the company: this result seems to be consistent with the policy of s. 438 because, if income can be accumulated by the trustees without attracting the higher rates, there is no harm in it being accumulated by the company in which the trustees hold shares. It should perhaps be mentioned that s. 438 (2) (*b*) prevents the obvious device of making capital advances to the child while the income is being accumulated free of tax at the higher rates, by providing that any sums paid under the settlement shall be deemed to be paid as income except to the extent that they exceed the aggregate available income.

Income contingently accumulated for the child is not taken into account in deciding whether the parent is entitled to the ordinary child allowance against the parent's own income tax, so that, if the child's income from other sources does not exceed £115 per annum, the full claim is available.

Express powers can be given to the trustees to apply income for the maintenance, education or benefit of the infant as they think fit and to accumulate any surplus income. The advantage of an express power is that accumulation can be authorised for a period of twenty-one years from the making of the settlement (see p. 38), but if it is not desired to accumulate after the beneficiary comes of age it is satisfactory to rely on the powers implied by s. 31 of the Trustee Act, 1925, in which references to the age of twenty-one should be read as eighteen in connection with settlements made on or after 1st January, 1970, when s. 1 of the Family Law Reform Act, 1969, came into force. If it becomes necessary in any particular year to draw on the income for the infant's maintenance or education, the only penalty is that this part of the income will be treated as the settlor's under ss. 437–444. The accumulation of any surplus income that can be saved is not prejudiced, nor are the accumulations of other years. By s. 16 of the Finance Act, 1973, accumulated income is subject to income tax at the additional rate as well as the basic rate.

Technical Education and Vacation Earnings

A very limited exception to the principle that a father cannot obtain tax relief for the cost of educating his infant child is provided by s. 133. The section allows a trader to make payments for the purpose of technical education related to that trade at a university or an approved technical college and to charge the payments as expenses of the trade. It was held in *Wickmar* v. *Berry* [1963] 1 W.L.R. 1026, that a farmer paying fees to an agricultural college for the education of his own son could rely on this section. Unfortunately, it is one of the few sections that apply to a trade but not a profession.

In *Mapp* v. *Oram* (1969), 45 T.C. 651, it was held by the House of Lords that vacation earnings of a child, which were non-taxable because earned abroad and never remitted, could not be counted as income of the child so as to reduce the child allowance of the parent.

CAPITAL GAINS TAX

On creation of the infant settlement the settlor will be deemed to have disposed at market value of the entire settled property under s. 25 (2) of the Finance Act, 1965, and will have to pay capital gains tax on any chargeable gains thrown up as a result. This will call for some care in choosing the assets to be settled, the considerations being the same as those discussed on p. 17 in relation to outright gifts. On future disposals by the trustees they will not have the right of an individual under s. 21 to pay income tax in any year on one-half of his chargeable gains up to £5,000, plus any excess over that figure, if this is less than capital gains tax. This will not usually be any deterrent, because people who can afford to accumulate income under an infant settlement will not often stand to gain by s. 21. The exemption for private residences is not necessarily lost by putting property into a settlement, because s. 29 (9) permits the trustees and a beneficiary entitled to occupation under the terms of the settlement to join forces in claiming exemption. This relief is extended in practice to cases where the beneficiary is entitled to the whole income from the property and is permitted by the trustees to occupy it, for example pending the carrying out of a trust for sale.

After the creation of the settlement, the trustees will be responsible for capital gains tax on any particular assets they realise in the course of changing investments, just as any other owner would be. Apart from this, the next occasion when capital gains tax strikes is when a beneficiary becomes absolutely entitled to the settled property as against the trustees, otherwise than on the death of a life tenant. The trustees are then deemed to have disposed of the whole fund under s. 25 (3) and must account for tax on any gains by reference to the base value of the assets. It is important to remember here that trustees have the right (referred to earlier on p. 18) under para. 4 of Sched. 10 to the Finance Act, 1965, as amended by s. 117 of the Finance Act, 1972, to pay the tax on deemed disposals by instalments over eight years in the case of certain assets which would be difficult to realise. The assets to which this right applies are land, or an estate or interest in land, unquoted shares and assets which were used immediately before the disposal exclusively for the purposes of a trade, profession or vocation. It is no longer necessary to prove hardship, and payment by instalments is now of right instead of, as formerly, in the discretion of the Board. Tax deferred in this way bears interest under the not very onerous provisions of ss. 86 and 89 of the Taxes Management Act, 1970, which call for interest at 6 per cent. net, but only if the total tax in question exceeds £1,000. If the assets are later disposed of for valuable consideration the tax and interest become due and payable forthwith. This is so whether or not the subsequent disposal was by the original donee or beneficiary.

Accumulated income is not in itself liable to capital gains tax, because of the general principle that taxable income must be excluded from chargeable gains, but if the income is invested a chargeable gain may be produced by those investments.

A curious possibility has emerged from the decision in *Glyn's Executor & Trustee Co.* v. *Tomlinson* (1969), 45 T.C. 600. By s. 22 (5) trustees holding for a person absolutely entitled or *who would be so entitled but for being an infant* are treated as his creatures and their acts are his. In particular the assets cease to be settled property for capital gains tax. The Court of Appeal held that the words in italics did not include an infant entitled contingently on attaining majority, but referred to someone with a vested interest whose infancy was the sole bar to giving the trustees a good receipt.

This implies that if the property vests in a beneficiary before he attains his majority, there is no deemed disposal by the trustees at that time, because s. 25 (3) does not contain the words in italics. Nor does s. 25 (3) apply when the beneficiary later attains majority, because the assets ceased to be settled property at the time of vesting. In fact, the deemed disposal under s. 25 (3) can be avoided altogether by making the assets vest in the infant shortly before he attains eighteen.

Once the trustees have become bare trustees under s. 22 (5), the actual transfer of assets to the beneficiary is not a chargeable disposal, although in certain circumstances the costs of breaking a settlement and transferring the assets may be allowable expenditure for the purposes of the deemed disposal under s. 25 (3) (*Commissioners of Inland Revenue* v. *Chubb's Settlement Trustee* [1971] T.R. 197). If the trustees have to realise assets, any gain will be chargeable on the beneficiary and not the trustees, which means that the beneficiary can claim the alternative rate of tax applicable to individuals under s. 21.

CHAPTER V

DISCRETIONARY TRUSTS

THE usefulness of the discretionary trust for saving estate duty was reduced, but by no means eliminated, by the Finance Act, 1969. The main advantages of the discretionary trust at present are as follows:

(1) Under the rules described later, the liability of the settled fund to estate duty on the death of a member of the family, who dies after the settlor, depends on whether he has received benefits. The powers of the trustees to accumulate income, and to distribute income or capital as they think fit among the family, give the trustees a chance to postpone estate duty by withholding distribution or to minimise it by distributing to those whose estates are likely to attract least duty.

Estate duty on the settlor's own death is not directly affected by the use of a discretionary trust. If the settlement operates to reduce the duty payable on the settlor's death, it will do so, like any other gift *inter vivos*, because it was made outside the requisite period.

(2) The income of the settlement can be applied by the trustees acting under their discretion in the best interests of the family as a whole, having regard to the different tax positions of its members. It is impossible when a trust is formed to foresee what the needs of the various beneficiaries will be in thirty or forty years' time, but the flexibility of a discretionary trust may avoid a share of income being heavily taxed in the hands of the beneficiary who least needs it.

(3) The income can be accumulated free of tax at the higher rates during any of the accumulation periods allowed by law.

(4) As with ordinary infant settlements (which may, of course, be discretionary) the shares in a family trading company are often the most readily available subject for a discretionary trust, and if a substantial proportion of the shares are settled in this way, it may be difficult for the Board of Inland Revenue to make an effective apportionment for the higher rates of tax of the close company's income. Alternatively it may be desirable for the trustees themselves, with suitable provisions in the trust deed, to carry on a business so that the profits are liable to income tax instead of corporation tax.

Form of Trust

The form of the discretionary trust was revolutionised by the decision of the House of Lords in *McPhail* v. *Doulton* [1970] 2 W.L.R. 1110. Before that decision, most full-scale discretionary trusts were based on a distinction which has been held in various cases, now overruled, to exist between trusts and powers. It was said that there were two different rules to observe. The first was that the objects of a trust must be certain; the second that the objects of a mere power need only be identifiable, which meant it was unnecessary to be able to say at any particular time who were all the possible objects of the power so long as any candidate for inclusion could be recognised. Relying on these two principles, the settlor used to create two classes of beneficiaries; the narrower class consisted of his children and issue and their spouses, and the wider class included these people but also took in others whom the testator wished to benefit, such as employees and ex-employees of his business and their dependants and various bodies which might or might not be charities. The trustees were then given a power to pay income to any member of the wider class, any remaining balance of income to be held on trust for the narrower class. The capital was dealt with in the same way, the trustees having a power to release capital among members of the wider class with an ultimate trust in favour of those members of the narrower class who might be in existence at the end of the perpetuity period.

The House of Lords held in *McPhail* v. *Doulton* that all this was unnecessary; there is only one test of certainty, which applies to both discretionary trusts and powers, and this is the more lenient one of whether any candidate who presents himself can be recognised as being or not being a member of the class of discretionary objects. If the trustees can tell a sheep from a goat, they no longer need to know all their sheep, which means that the two classes of the traditional form of trust can be amalgamated. In *Re Saxone Shoe Co. Ltd.'s Trust Deed* [1962] 1 W.L.R. 943, the use of the word "dependant" was held not to be too vague as the description of an object, while the decision in *Re Gulbenkian's Settlement* [1968] Ch. 126 shows that the court is allowed to construe an ambiguous description so that it makes sense.

These developments were discussed by the Court of Appeal in *Re Baden's Deed Trusts* (*No.* 2) [1972] 2 All E.R. 1304, where it was held that there was no *conceptual uncertainty* about discretionary trusts in favour of either "dependants" or "relatives" and any *evidential difficulty* there might be in establishing the claim of a candidate did not invalidate the trusts. There is no objection to the trustees being given power to add to the list by nomination, but for tax reasons the settlor and any wife of his should be excluded from all possibility of being nominated (see p. 42).

Accumulations

By s. 164 of the Law of Property Act, 1925, as amended by s. 13 of the Perpetuities and Accumulations Act, 1964, the only periods for accumulation of income permissible in a settlement *inter vivos* are—

(*a*) the life of the grantor or settlor, or

(*b*) the duration of the minority or respective minorities only of any person or persons who under the limitations of the instrument directing the accumulations would, for the time being, if of full age, be entitled to the income directed to be accumulated, or

(*c*) a term of twenty-one years from the making of the disposition, or

(*d*) the duration of the minority or respective minorities of any person or persons in being at that date.

The difference between (*d*) and (*b*) is that the infants referred to in (*d*) do not need to be beneficiaries. The original section contains two other periods, closely corresponding to (*c*) and (*d*), which have been held to be applicable only to a settlement by will.

The section applies to a mere power to accumulate as well as to a trust, and it would obviously be unwise to give a power to accumulate income during the life of the settlor, because on his death a proportion of the fund corresponding to the income actually accumulated would be deemed to pass under para. (iv) of the new s. 2 (1) (*b*) of the Finance Act, 1894 (see ss. 36 (2) and 37 (3) of the Finance Act, 1969).

If any period is chosen, apart from the permitted ones, it is liable to be cut down by the premature death of the settlor during the period, and if this happens the effect is exactly the same for estate duty purposes as if accumulation for the life of the settlor had originally been directed. A full discretionary trust today usually includes a general power to accumulate income for the first twenty-one years, as well as power to accumulate income appointed to a particular beneficiary during his minority.

The Perpetuities and Accumulations Act, 1964, also provides in s. 1 a convenient perpetuity period of eighty years, but if this is to be used it must be expressly referred to.

ESTATE DUTY

The Finance Act, 1969, introduced a new system for charging estate duty on settled property by reference to the deceased's beneficial interest in possession during the seven years before his death. Discretionary trusts were brought within the new system, but the special nature of these trusts required a special solution. Since it was obviously impossible to treat every discretionary object as having a beneficial interest in the settled property for the purpose of charging duty on his death, the basic test adopted was the receipt of income benefits during the seven-year period. On the death after 15th April, 1969, of a discretionary object who has received the whole of the income of the settled property during the seven years before his death, the whole of the property is liable to estate duty under s. 2 (1) (*b*) (iii) of the Finance Act, 1894, inserted by s. 36 (2) of the Finance Act, 1969. If the deceased received only part of the total income during the period, a proportionate part of the settled property is liable (s. 37 (3) of the Finance Act, 1969).

This general rule has to be qualified in various ways:

(1) No account is to be taken of benefits received on or before 15th April, 1963. The object is to prevent trustees having to produce records for more than six years before Budget Day, 1969.

(2) The general rule assumes that the deceased was still an eligible discretionary object at his death. If he ceased to be eligible, or the property ceased to be subject to the trust, within the seven years before the death, then a different seven-year period has to be taken for the purpose of calculating the income benefits. This is the seven-year period ending when the deceased ceased to be eligible or the property ceased to be settled. In other words, it will be possible in this case for benefits received as long ago as fourteen years before the death to be taken into account, subject always to the starting point of 15th April, 1963. The reason is that it would be unreal to average the benefits over the seven-year period immediately before death, if during the latter part of that period the deceased could not possibly have benefited.

(3) If the deceased ceased to be eligible, or the property ceased to be settled, more than seven years before his death, there may still be an estate duty liability if the deceased had not been entirely excluded from possession and enjoyment of the property, and from any benefit by contract or otherwise, for the whole of the seven years before his death. Here the seven-year period for the purpose of calculating the income benefits is the seven-year period ending when the deceased ceased to be eligible or the property ceased to be settled, however long ago that was, but subject to the starting point of 15th April, 1963.

(4) What have been called income benefits include a capital distribution to the deceased, to the extent that

income which could have been paid to him under the discretion has been accumulated instead, and also the value of any benefit by way of use and enjoyment of any part of the settled property.

(5) Any settled property to which the deceased became absolutely entitled before his death is not charged with duty under s. 2(1) (*b*) by reason of anything that happened while it was still settled (para. 2 of Sched. 17 to the Finance Act, 1969). This prevents a double charge on property that has become part of the free estate.

(6) Schedule 17 also preserves for settled property the benefit of certain general reliefs, such as the surviving spouse exemption, quick succession relief, and taper relief where the deceased's interest ceased during the fifth, sixth or seventh year before death.

Since the extent of the charge to estate duty on the settled property depends on the proportion borne by the deceased's income benefits to the trust income during a seven-year period, it is essential to know the basis on which trust income should be calculated. The Board of Inland Revenue has issued an extremely important statement of practice on this point, which is reproduced in Appendix C. (See also *British Tax Review* [1970] 283.)

The way in which estate duty is charged on discretionary trusts has to be kept in mind by the trustees when exercising their powers. The principle is that an income benefit to a discretionary object will give rise to a claim to estate duty on the settled property on the death of *that discretionary object* within seven years, while a capital advance may give rise to a claim on the death within seven years of *some other discretionary object* who has had an income benefit within the seven years before the advance since the property advanced ceases to be settled within rule (2) on p. 40. It also follows that if a discretionary object wishes to cease benefiting, in order that the risk of the settled property suffering estate duty on his death may be reduced, it is better for him not to disclaim his "interest", but simply to ask the trustees not to give him any more income benefits. If he disclaims, he ceases to be eligible under rule (2) and, if he had had income benefits during the seven years before the disclaimer, these continue to be relevant to an estate duty charge until the expiry of another seven-year period after the disclaimer. If, on the other hand, he remains an eligible discretionary object, but without drawing any income, each of the past benefits will drop out of account as soon as seven years have passed from the date on which it was received.

INCOME TAX

By s. 448, if the settlor or the wife or husband of the settlor is an object of the discretion, the whole income of the settlement is treated for tax purposes as the income of the settlor, and it is therefore necessary to persuade the settlor that he should exclude not only himself but his wife from any benefit under the settlement. Section 448 provides an exception in the case of a power in favour of the settlor or the wife or husband of the settlor which cannot be exercised within six years from the commencement of the settlement, in which case the section does not apply so long as the power cannot be exercised.

There is an awkward decision in *Commissioners of Inland Revenue* v. *Tennant* (1942), 24 T.C. 215, under a section similarly referring to the wife or husband of the settlor (actually the predecessor of s. 447 mentioned in Chapter III) where it was held that the settlement was ineffective because the settlor, a widow, had a power of appointment which might be exercised in favour of her husband should she re-marry. The implications of this decision are enormous since in certain events almost anyone in the world might marry almost anyone else provided only that the sexes were right. In an important letter published in the *Law Society's Gazette* for January, 1959, the Board of Inland Revenue have stated that they do not regard the decision in *Commissioners of Inland Revenue* v. *Tennant* as applying unless the settlor is unmarried at the material time or the terms of the settlement indicate a specific intention that the future wife or husband of the settlor might be enabled to benefit. In practice, therefore, a general power of appointment will only be fatal while the settlor is unmarried. In spite of this helpful concession, it is obviously wise to provide specifically in the settlement that neither the settlor nor any present or future spouse of the settlor can benefit.

Commissioners of Inland Revenue v. *Bernstein* (1969), 39 T.C. 391, is a case in which the settlor actually did marry one of the beneficiaries. Under the trusts of the settlement his wife could only benefit during his lifetime if the power of advancement under s. 32 of the Trustee Act, 1925, was applicable. The court held that it was not applicable because, although it was not expressly barred, there was a trust for accumulation during the settlor's lifetime which was inconsistent with the statutory power. While this is a useful decision to rely on if necessary, it would be better in a similar case to provide expressly that s. 32 should not apply to the settlement.

It is sometimes asked whether, if the wife of the settlor cannot be included as the object of a discretionary trust, it is not possible to benefit at least his widow. From the point of view of income tax this is unexceptionable (*Vestey's Executors* v. *Commissioners of Inland Revenue* (1949), 31 T.C. 1), and the danger that the extension of the class of objects at the moment of the settlor's death might cause a passing of the property for estate duty was removed by the Finance Act, 1969, with its new scheme for charging estate duty on settled property by reference to beneficial interests rather than change of title. In addition to s. 448, the other statutory requirements for settlements in general, mentioned in Chapter III, must be observed.

Investment Income Surcharge on Accumulation

With the abolition of earned income relief which came into effect with the unified tax system on 6th April, 1973, provision is made for an additional rate of income tax on investment income, colloquially known as the "Investment Income Surcharge". By the Finance Act, 1973, s. 16, this is made applicable to income accumulated in the hands of trustees, or which is payable at their discretion whether or not there is power to accumulate. In the case of individuals the surcharge applies to investment income over a certain amount, which for 1973/74 is £2000, but in the case of trustees' income under s. 16, it applies to all their income after defraying expenses. In cases where income is deemed to be that of the settlor under any of the anti-avoidance provisions, or is exempt, as in the case of charities, the surcharge is not applied.

By s. 17 of the same Act, when a payment under discretionary trusts is made to any beneficiary in the form of income, it is treated as a net amount corresponding to a gross amount from which the tax at the basic rate and investment income surcharge have been deducted. The amount of these notional deductions is treated as income tax paid by the beneficiary and as income tax assessable on the trustees, who may set it off against tax for which they may already be liable in respect of the income. For this last purpose, tax in respect of income accumulated and available for distribution at the end of the year 1972/73 is treated as being two thirds of the net amount of that income. It is interesting that s. 17 makes the payment income for the year in which it was paid. This has hitherto been in doubt so far as the beneficiary's income was concerned if the payment was made out of income of previous years.

Dividends and Annual Payments as Earned Income

Where the shares of a family trading company have been settled and the trustees are given power to pay the income to a member of the family so long as he is engaged in the management of the company, it was sometimes possible to obtain earned income relief in respect of the dividends. The authority for this surprising proposition is the Court of Appeal decision in *White* v. *Franklin* [1965] 1 All E.R. 692. Under the new unified system it will be open to anyone in this position to contend that the investment income surcharge does not apply to such dividends.

Another possibility of making payments under a settlement, whether discretionary or not, which used to attract earned income relief has been firmly established by the House of Lords. In *Dale* v. *Commissioners of Inland Revenue* [1954] A.C. 11, it was held that annuity payments provided by a will for a trustee with onerous duties were emoluments of his office as trustee and accordingly qualified as earned income. (The Finance Act, 1969, abolished the estate duty exemption which formerly applied when the deceased's interest was as holder of an office, but the Board of Inland Revenue consider that the part of the trust property required to produce so much of a trustee's annuity as represented reasonable remuneration for his services is exempt from duty on his death, under s. 3 of the Finance Act, 1894, on the ground of purchase.)

Both these decisions are worth study with a view to application in suitable cases, but it is not suggested that they authorise any artificial conversion of unearned into earned income.

CAPITAL GAINS TAX

When s. 59 of the Finance Act, 1971, abolished the charge to capital gains tax on death in most cases, the rule under which trustees of a settlement without life interests were deemed to dispose of the trust assets every fifteen years was also abolished. Schedule 12 applies the new scheme to discretionary trusts in the following way. Whenever the settled property is chargeable with estate duty under s. 2 (1) (*b*) (iii) of the Finance Act, 1894, on the death of a discretionary object who has received income benefits, a portion of each of the assets comprised in the settled property aquires a new base value equal to market value at the date of the death, but without any capital gains tax being payable. The portion of each of the assets to acquire a new base in this way is arrived at by asking what was the value on which estate duty was chargeable compared with the market value of the whole of the settled property at the time of the death. By this somewhat inconvenient method of attributing to each separate asset, in the capital gains tax sense, a proportionately uplifted base value, the principle is preserved that payment of estate duty should wipe out any chargeable gain accrued up to death.

A discretionary trust is in the same position as any other settlement with regard to the settlor's liability to capital gains tax on assets transferred to the trustees and the trustees' liability on changes of investment (p. 33). On the termination of a pure discretionary trust, there will always be a potential charge to capital gains tax against the trustees, because by definition the termination will not be due to the death of a life tenant.

The head of the family, who is settling shares in the company he controls, may be able to reduce his capital gains tax on the deemed disposal by relying on s. 34 of the Finance Act, 1965. This section exempts from capital gains tax a maximum of £10,000 chargeable gains arising on the disposal of certain business assets included in a business, or part of a business, of which the owner disposes after reaching the age of sixty. The full exemption of £10,000 is only available if he waits until he is sixty-five and it is reduced by £2,000 for every year by which he falls short of this age. The disposal may be by sale or gift.

The retirement relief is available in respect of shares in a trading company, but only if it is the taxpayer's family company, which is arbitrarily defined by s. 34 (6), and he is a full-time working director. To fall within the definition the voting rights must be exercisable as to not less than 25 per cent. by the individual, or as to not less than 75 per cent. by the individual or a member of his family and as to not less than 10 per cent. by the individual himself. If the individual is to rely on the second leg of this definition because he retains somewhere between 10 per cent. and 25 per cent., it is essential that the rest of the 75 per cent. should be held by a member of his family. "Family" is defined in the usual way to include husband or wife and brother, sister, ancestor or lineal descendant of the individual or his wife, which means that shares already held by a settlement would not count towards the 75 per cent. unless the trustees were members of the family within this class. This may be a factor to be borne in mind when deciding on trustees, if the settlor is retaining some shares of the company which could be the subject of a claim under s. 34 on a subsequent disposal.

For s. 34 to apply the business must have been owned by the individual for at least ten years immediately before the disposal or, alternatively, the disposal must be of shares of a company which has been the individual's family company and of which he has been a full time working director during that period. The Finance Act, 1966, Sched. 10, para. 2 (3), caters for a case where a business is transferred to a company during the ten-year period and in practice relief is also allowed where the business has been transferred from one family company to another, provided that the shareholdings before and after the transfer were similar and there was no cessation for tax purposes.

In the case of business assets or shares which were held before 6th April, 1965, the benefit of time-apportionment can be claimed before the application of the s. 34 relief, so that the full amount of relief available in the circumstances is set against the part of the gain which is chargeable.

The privilege of postponing payment of tax in respect of disposals of land, non-quoted shares and business assets referred to earlier (pp. 18 and 34) may also be advantageous in these circumstances.

CHAPTER VI

SETTLEMENTS WITH REVERTER TO DISPONER

ESTATE DUTY

WHEN a settlor, which is all that disponer means, makes a simple settlement on a dependant for life, it would be hard if duty had to be paid on the property coming back to the settlor on the death of the life tenant. This hardship must have been noticed very quickly after the introduction of estate duty in 1894, because s. 15 of the Finance Act, 1896, gave an exemption which is still in force.

Although the exemption is not confined to husband and wife, its great attraction is the way it enables a husband to avoid estate duty on his property on the death of the first to die of his wife and himself, a more satisfactory arrangement than the surviving spouse exemption which only avoids duty on the second death.

Section 15 works like this. If a husband, having settled property on his wife for life, survives the gift by seven years, the only thing to pass on his death is the reversionary interest; his executors can exercise the election under s. 7 (6) of the Finance Act, 1894, to defer duty on this until it falls into possession, which will be on the death of the wife. The subsequent death of the wife will attract no further duty, because the surviving spouse exemption applies, duty being treated as paid in respect of the settled property on the death of the husband even though the election to defer payment was exercised.

If on the other hand it is the wife who dies first, s. 15 exempts the property from duty when it reverts to the husband.

The conditions to be observed in order to obtain the benefit of the section are stringent:

(1) The life tenant must enter into possession of the life

interest and retain possession to the entire exclusion of the settlor or of any benefit to him by contract or otherwise. These words are familiar in connection with gifts *inter vivos* and should presumably be construed in the same way, except that s. 35 (3) of the Finance Act, 1959, which brings associated operations into the definition of benefits reserved on a gift does not apply to the s. 15 exemption; it would of course apply if the question were whether the original gift in settlement was liable to duty on the death of the settlor after the seven-year period.

(2) The interests created by the settlement must be confined to the life interest and the reversion, except that life interests for more than one person, whether joint or several or even in succession, are permitted.

(3) The settled property must not be property of which the life tenant was competent to dispose at any time before the creation of the settlement. This rules out, for example, a settlement by a wife of property which her husband had previously given to her, however long ago.

(4) The exemption does not apply if the settled property is itself a life interest of the settlor under another settlement, a condition introduced to prevent avoidance of the 1969 scheme for charging estate duty on settled property under the substituted s. 2 (1) (*b*) of the Finance Act, 1894.

(5) On the death of the life tenant the property must revert to the settlor himself and not to an assignee of any description; the exemption does not apply if the property reverts to the executors of a settlor who has died before the life tenant, although in the case of husband and wife, as already mentioned, the surviving spouse exemption would then be available on the death of the life tenant.

Useful though the exemption is, it may not apply to cases where husband and wife both have assets and both wish to postpone duty until the death of the second to die. If the assets all originated from one spouse, a settlement by the other would not qualify for the exemption because of condition (3). Even if the assets had been separately acquired by the husband and the wife, there would be a problem about mutual settlements with reverter to disponer, since each settlor might be considered to have obtained a benefit by contract or otherwise in the shape of the other settlement, with the result that exemption would be lost under condition (1).

A solution in these cases may be found by relying on the exemption for purchase in s. 3 of the Finance Act, 1894, rather than on s. 15 of the Finance Act, 1896. If the husband sells to the wife a reversionary interest in his assets taking effect on his death, the consideration being a reversionary interest granted to him by his wife in her assets and taking effect on her death, then it seems that on the death of the first to die his assets would pass to the other by purchase and would be exempt from duty under s. 3. The reversionary interest in the other's assets would pass on the death of the first to die, but his executors could exercise the election to defer payment of duty until the reversion fell in on the second death. The assets to be dealt with in this way by each party would have to be decided on actuarial advice, so that the values of the two reversionary interests were equal at the time of the transaction.

CAPITAL GAINS TAX

Since a gift in settlement is required if advantage is to be taken of the exemption for reverter to disponer, it is not possible on the initial arrangements to take advantage also of the capital gains tax exemption on outright disposals between husband and wife under para. 20 of Sched. 7 to the Finance Act, 1965. As a result of the Finance Act, 1971, there will be no capital gains tax on the death of the life tenant, whether a surviving spouse or not, reverter to disponer being one of the rare occasions where the capital gains tax exemption under s. 59 and Sched. 12 applies even though estate duty is not charged on the same death. But the gain up to the date of reverter is not wiped out and the disponer takes the property back with the trustees' base value.

CHAPTER VII

DEEDS OF COVENANT

THE familiar deed of covenant is a method of transferring from one person to another the legal title to income which in the absence of special legislation would always be recognised for tax purposes, resulting in an over-all saving if the transferee pays tax at a lower rate than the transferor. The first restriction is contained in s. 434, by which a deed of covenant not made for valuable and sufficient consideration is ineffective for all tax purposes if the period during which the income is payable cannot exceed six years, but it would be a mistake to assume, having considered s. 434, that there are no other statutory difficulties in the way. The remainder of Pt. XVI of the Act (ss. 434–459) deals with settlements, and the word "settlement" can apply just as much to a deed of covenant as to the settlement of capital which lawyers more usually associate with the name.

Before considering Pt. XVI, it is necessary to recall that the machinery of a deed of covenant works, if it works at all, because the payments under it are annual payments falling within Case III of Schedule D. An annual payment was defined as a pure income payment in *Howe* v. *Commissioners of Inland Revenue* [1919] 2 K.B. 336, where a claim to deduct tax from annual life insurance premiums was unsuccessful. It would not include, for example, payments under a covenant made direct with a butcher in consideration of a supply of meat, because they would not be pure income in his hands but would form part of his gross takings. The House of Lords held in *British Commonwealth International Newsfilm Agency, Ltd.* v. *Mahany* [1963] 1 W.L.R. 69 that payments under covenant by Rank Organisation, Ltd. and the B.B.C. to subsidise losses of the Newsfilm Agency were trading receipts of the Newsfilm Agency and not annual payments. The same applies to a covenant made with a school for payment of fees, but if an employer covenants to pay sums to trustees to be applied at their discretion for the education of children of employees, an amount voted to a child will be the child's own income and the payments by the employer will rank as annual payments (*Barclays Bank, Ltd.* v. *Naylor* [1961] Ch. 7). Since the introduction of corporation tax, the scheme adopted in the *Barclays Bank* case would not be advantageous to a company for the reasons explained on p. 53.

It was said in *Commissioners of Inland Revenue* v. *National Book League* [1957] Ch. 488 that annual payments must also be made without conditions or counter-stipulations. The National Book League failed to establish that subscriptions paid by its members under covenant were annual payments, because the members derived certain advantages from the subscriptions which could not be dismissed on the principle of *de minimis non curat lex.*

In *Campbell* v. *Commissioners of Inland Revenue* [1970] A.C. 77, the House of Lords considered that the National Book League case was rightly decided on its facts, since the payments were simply club subscriptions, but that conditions or counter-stipulations do not necessarily deprive payments of the character of pure income. The actual decision in *Campbell* was that payments under covenant to a charitable trust, which it had been agreed the trust should use to buy a tutorial business from the covenantor, were received by the trustees not as income but as capital.

As a result of these cases, *pure income* must be understood as something which—

(*a*) is taxable in the hands of the recipient as income, but

(*b*) is not received as gross trading income.

Where an annual payment is made wholly out of income charged to income tax, s. 52 comes into play and the payer is entitled to deduct tax at the basic rate for the year in which the payment becomes due. The payer puts the tax deducted into his own pocket as a way of recouping the income tax he has suffered on an equivalent slice of his own income, and having obtained relief in this way he is not allowed to deduct the payment from his total income, except for the purpose of reducing tax payable at the additional or higher rates. The recipient on the other hand receives a payment which has already been taxed at the basic rate, but he can make a reclaim in respect of the tax deducted if his allowances and reliefs have not been fully exhausted by other income, a certificate of deduction of tax being supplied by the payer for this purpose.

Section 53 applies where an annual payment is not payable wholly out of taxed income. Here the payer must deduct tax at the basic rate in force at the time of actual payment and must account to the Revenue for the whole of the tax deducted, or for a proportion of it if the payment was made partly out of taxed income and partly out of capital. To make an annual payment out of capital would be to turn capital into income, contrary to all the rules of tax planning.

Since a company's profits are not liable to income tax, a company making an annual payment is always in the s. 53 position and must account to the Revenue for basic rate tax on the gross amount of the payment. Under the corporation tax system, the only way in which a company can obtain relief for an annual payment is to deduct the gross amount from its total profits as a "charge on income" under s. 248. But a payment is not a charge on income unless it is made under a liability incurred for a valuable and sufficient consideration or is a donation to charity under a seven-year covenant.

It was held in *Ball* v. *National and Grindlays Bank, Ltd.* [1971] 3 all E.R. 485, that incurred "for" a valuable and sufficient consideration means incurred "in return for" rather than "with a view to", and therefore the business advantage to be obtained by making payments under a deed of covenant to trustees of a scheme for educating the children of employees of the company was not consideration within the meaning of the section. It was also held in *Commissioners of Inland Revenue* v. *Educational Grants Association, Ltd.* [1967] Ch. 993, that a trust for the education of children connected with a particular company is not a charity, although a trust for poor employees of the company may be charitable (*Dingle* v. *Turner* [1972] 1 All E.R. 878).

It follows from these decisions that a company cannot obtain relief for covenanted payments under a scheme for educating employees' children, although an individual employer or partnership may still do so. It would be better for a company with such a scheme to make voluntary payments to the trustees which might be allowed as wholly and exclusively laid out for the purposes of the trade.

Statutory Restrictions

(1) The best known restriction on deeds of covenant is that contained in s. 434 which lays down the minimum period of six years and this period, with the addition of a margin for safety, has given rise to the well known phrase "a seven-year covenant". The safety margin is advisable because it is easy to make mistakes with the six-year period, which has been held to run from the date of the first payment to the date of the last, irrespective of the number of years intended to be covered. Another difficulty is that any backdating of the first payment will not be recognised for tax purposes, and the first payment will be considered to be due not earlier than the date of the deed. These rules are worth illustrating by the facts in *Commissioners of Inland Revenue* v. *St. Luke's Hostel Trustees* (1930), 15 T.C. 682. A subscriber covenanted to pay the hostel £10 annually during the term of seven years from 6th April, 1926, the first payment to be made on 31st December, 1926, and subsequent payments on 31st December in each year. Unfortunately the deed was not executed until 3rd February, 1927, the first payment being actually made on 4th February, 1927. The Court of Appeal held that the period during which the income was payable ran from 3rd February, 1927, to 31st December, 1932, and was therefore one which could not exceed six years.

On the other hand, a deed need not in fact last for six years if it is capable of doing so, and this is why it can be made terminable on the earlier death of either party. Provided that the deed creates a legally binding obligation, it does not matter that the covenantee decides not to take steps to enforce it or even agrees to its cancellation before the six years have run. Payments made before the cancellation are not affected, although it would, of course, be wrong for a deed to be entered into with the deliberate intention of agreeing to cancel it at a certain date.

(2) By s. 445 sums payable by the settlor or his wife under a revocable deed of covenant are treated as still forming part of the settlor's income, except that if the power of revocation cannot be exercised within six years from the time when the first payment becomes payable the section does not apply so long as the power is not exercisable. This provision corresponds closely with s. 446 applying to revocable capital settlements (p. 22).

(3) Section 450 is another section which applies mainly to deeds of covenant and not to capital settlements. The effect of the section is that, where sums are paid under covenant to trustees who accumulate the payments, the settlor is not allowed to deduct the sums in computing his liability to the higher rates of tax, at any rate to the extent that they remain undistributed in the hands of the trustees at the end of the tax year. This is not particularly important because s. 457 would normally prevent the settlor obtaining any relief against higher rates of tax, but s. 450 goes on to provide that no relief shall be given on account of tax paid in respect of the income undistributed at the end of the year, which means that if the income is distributed to the beneficiaries in a later year they cannot obtain any repayment of tax to which they would otherwise be entitled by reason of their personal allowances.

The section applies only where the income is held by the trustees on a discretionary trust or contingently for some beneficiary, because income which has vested in a beneficiary belongs to him, whether the trustees have actually paid it over or not. Where the section does apply, it is essential that trustees should take care to make a full distribution before 5th April in each year.

(4) Section 457 is not confined to deeds of covenant, but its main application is to annual payments because of the exception in favour of income from property of which the settlor has divested himself absolutely. The forerunner of the section was passed as a result of the decision of the House of Lords in *Commissioners of Inland Revenue* v. *Duke of Westminster* [1936] A.C. 1, where the taxpayer successfully arranged for his servants to accept payments under covenant in lieu of wages with

the result that the total gross amounts were allowable against his surtax. The decision in the *Duke of Westminster's* case still stands so far as it concerns the general principle of deeds of covenant and is regarded as the high-water mark of the doctrine that form is more important than substance. Section 457, which only applies to tax at the additional or higher rates, in its original form prevented any effective transfer of income to servants, solicitors or agents of the settlor or their children or to any nominee. It also prevented the transfer of income to any person who was not an individual and, although charities were nowhere mentioned in the section, its principal result was to avoid any surtax benefit in the case of deeds of covenant in favour of charities. The saving in favour of individuals was later removed with the result that s. 457 applies, but still only for the purposes of tax at the additional or higher rates, to all covenants made on or after 7th April, 1965, except for certain annual payments made to a retired partner or his widow or dependants under a partnership agreement, or to a vendor or his widow or dependants in connection with the purchase of a business, or under settlements arising out of matrimonial disputes. Since the first two of these excepted cases are limited to liabilities incurred for full consideration, while the third will also be far from voluntary as a rule, it may be wondered why it was necessary to create the exceptions. The draftsman seems to have taken the view, contrary to the decision in *Bulmer* v. *Commissioners of Inland Revenue* [1967] Ch. 145, that "settlements" within s. 457 can include arrangements made on commercial terms.

There are also the following provisions mentioned in Chapter III, which apply both to capital settlements and deeds of covenant and may be vital to the success of a deed which has survived all the other hazards:

(5) By s. 437, a settlement in favour of an infant child of the settlor is ineffective for tax purposes. Income accumulated under an irrevocable settlement of capital is excluded, but this loophole is not available for payments under a deed of covenant (s. 438 (2) (*a*)).

(6) Under s. 448, income paid to trustees on discretionary

trusts will be deemed to remain the income of the settlor, if the settlor or the spouse of the settlor is one of the discretionary objects.

Use of Deed of Covenant

With the above obstacles in mind it will be seen that the chief uses of the deed of covenant are for saving income tax in the following circumstances:

(1) It can be used to transfer income from a settlor to a member of his family, other than a spouse or an unmarried child of the settlor who is under eighteen. One factor to be remembered is that the child allowance may continue beyond the age of majority if the child is still receiving full-time education. If the income of a child is more than £115 the child allowance is reduced by £1 for every £1 of the child's own income over that figure. Since there is no objection to a covenant for a fluctuating amount, provided the covenant contains the formula for fixing the payments, it is possible to have a covenant for the maximum amount in each year which will not cause the child allowance to be reduced.

(2) Deeds of covenant in favour of charities are very frequently employed. Since the charity is not liable to income tax, the full amount deducted from the payments can be reclaimed and there is a maximum advantage.

(3) In the case of a business carried on by an individual or by partners, it is often advisable for payments which may not be allowable as expenses of the trade to be made by deed of covenant. If this is done, the business obtains tax relief by deduction at source and no question arises as to whether the payments have been wholly and exclusively incurred for the purposes of the trade under s. 130. A *company* must account to the Revenue for the tax deducted, and the gross amount is only allowable against corporation tax if the payments are made under a liability incurred for valuable and sufficient consideration, or under a seven-year covenant in favour of charity.

(4) A deed of covenant under which the payments are held by trustees on discretionary trusts is not necessarily

ineffective for tax purposes, but the trustees must be careful to distribute all the income before the end of the tax year in order that s. 450 may not apply.

(5) Tax at the additional or higher rates also can be saved in the three cases exempted from s. 457, which relate to payments made under partnership agreements, under agreements for the acquisition of a business, and settlements connected with matrimonial proceedings or separations. Partnership agreements are dealt with in greater detail in Chapter XIII.

Tax Reclaim

The destination of the income tax reclaim depends on the wording of the deed. The simplest form of wording is a covenant to pay the gross sum decided by the parties from which it follows automatically that tax at the basic rate is deducted whether this deduction is referred to in the deed or not. Where the parties have decided on a net sum it is usual to employ a formula; if the wording is to pay "such a sum as after deduction of tax at the basic rate (or current rate) will leave £X", the amount of tax reclaimed by the covenantee will belong to him. The authority for this is *Re Jones* [1933] Ch. 842, with which should be contrasted the far less convenient rule in *Re Pettit* [1922] 2 Ch. 765. *Re Pettit* applies where there is no reference to basic rate or current rate, but the formula merely calls for the deduction of tax or income tax, which will be construed to mean the covenantee's personal rate of tax so that any reclaim made by him belongs to the covenantor and must be handed over. The decision in *Re Kingcome* [1936] Ch. 566 shows that in these circumstances the covenantee is under a duty to make the reclaim for the benefit of the covenantor.

The Royal Commission on the Taxation of Profits and Income in its final report (Cmd. 9474, 1955) recommended that the maker of a covenant in favour of a child, grandchild or other member of his family should be required to produce each year formal declarations by himself and the beneficiary as to the absence of any agreement or understanding for the return, direct or indirect, of any part of the benefit. In reply to a question in the

House of Commons on 30th July, 1959, the Chancellor of the Exchequer stated that the existence of conditions or counter-stipulations in regard to payments under any deed of covenant, whether the beneficiary was a member of the covenantor's family or not, prevented the deed from operating as a valid transfer of income for tax purposes—a statement which needs qualification since the decision in *Campbell* v. *Commissioners of Inland Revenue* (p. 52). He said that no legislative action was considered necessary but inspectors of taxes would be instructed to call for declarations on this point, a practice which is usually followed when claims are submitted.

Stamp Duty

Stamp duty on deeds of covenant was abolished by s. 64 of the Finance Act, 1971.

CHAPTER VIII

COMPANIES

BEFORE considering in Chapters IX to XI how far various kinds of company can be used for saving tax, it is necessary to look at the tax position of companies in general which has been radically altered by the Finance Act, 1972.

As in the old system of company taxation, income tax has no general application to company profits which are charged to corporation tax instead. Under the new as well as the old system company profits for this purpose include both taxable income and capital gains, but capital gains are now to be charged at a lower rate than income. This rate will be fixed by Parliament from time to time and at the time of writing has not been fixed for 1973/1974, which is the first year of operation of the new system. Capital gains tax as such still has no application to companies.

Dividends and other distributions of the company are now dealt with for taxation purposes in what may truthfully be called a revolutionary way. When "qualifying distributions" are made, advance corporation tax (ACT) becomes payable. "Qualifying distributions" are in fact most distributions under s. 233 except bonus redeemable share capital and bonus securities. ACT is calculated as a fraction of the amount of the distribution (the ACT rate) and can later be set off against the company's liability for corporation tax. The rate is fixed by Parliament annually and the recipient of the dividend is, if a United Kingdom resident or company, entitled to a tax credit of the same proportion of the distribution as the ACT rate. For the first year of operation of the system (1973/1974) the ACT rate is three-sevenths, so that the tax credit will be three-sevenths of the distribution. Tax will no longer be deducted from dividends under Schedule F, which in its old form is abolished and is replaced by a new Schedule F which charges dividends and distributions in the hands of the recipient. Thus, any distribution in respect of which a person or company is entitled to a tax credit is treated as representing income in his hands equal to the aggregate of the amount or value of the distribution and the amount of the tax credit, and income tax is charged on that total sum. Thus if a shareholder receives a dividend of £56 he is chargeable to income tax under Schedule F on £80 which is the amount of the dividend plus three-sevenths, or £24. He will be able to set off his tax credit of £24 against his tax liability at the basic rate. Assuming a basic rate of 30 per cent., the tax credit will exactly equal the basic rate income tax, leaving the shareholder liable only to the higher rates of income tax on the £80.

Company income is computed on ordinary income tax principles as are its chargeable gains on capital gains tax principles, except so far as these are expressly modified by the Acts. One important modification is that corporation tax is not assessed on a previous year basis, like income tax under Cases I and II of Schedule D, but on the actual profits of the company's accounting periods. This gets rid of all the complications arising from the special rules about the opening and closing years of a business under Schedule D, with their opportunities for avoidance and their corresponding anti-avoidance provisions. Capital losses cannot be set against income profits, and in fact income itself has to be dissected between the Schedules to prevent a company being better off in the matter of losses than an individual or a partnership. For instance, trading losses can be carried forward only against profits from the same trade, and Case VI losses can only be set against Case VI profits. But a company has one advantage and that is the right to set trading losses against capital gains of the same or the preceding accounting period.

"Distribution" is a technical word defined in s. 233, as amended by para. 2 of Sched. 22 to the Finance Act, 1972. Its importance lies in the fact that distributions are not allowed as deductions from company profits for corporation tax. An extended definition of distribution applies to close companies, which will be considered later, but for other companies the main examples of distributions are dividends, whether on ordinary or preference shares, capital dividends, distributions of assets *in specie*, issues of redeemable bonus shares, and bonus issues coupled with a reduction of capital. Neither a bonus issue of shares (non-redeemable), nor a reduction of capital, counts as a distribution so long as it stands alone. Payments or transfers *in specie* to a member in a winding up are not distributions, even if they exceed the nominal value of his shares; they will of course give rise to capital gains tax in the hands of the member under s. 22 (4) of the 1965 Act, if he receives more than the base value of his shares.

There are other aspects of income tax from which a company cannot keep entirely aloof. A company receiving an annual payment will receive it under deduction of income tax, and when it makes an annual payment to someone else it will deduct income tax. How do these transactions fit in with corporation tax?

If the company is the one making the payment, it is known as a "charge on income" and the gross amount is deductible from the company's profits, provided that the payment is made under a liability incurred for valuable and sufficient consideration or under a seven-year covenant in favour of a charity (s. 248). In any case the income tax deducted must be accounted for to the Revenue, which makes it important that a company should not enter into a seven-year covenant without being sure that it will be treated as a charge on income (see *Ball* v. *National and Grindlays Bank, Ltd.*, p. 53). If the company is receiving the annual payment, the gross amount has to be included in the profits liable to corporation tax.

The treatment of distributions received from another United Kingdom company has been adapted to the new system. Qualifying distributions received by a United Kingdom company plus the tax credits thereon are called franked investment income, and so far as the paying company is concerned are called franked payments. By s. 89 of the Finance Act, 1972, a company only pays ACT to the extent that its own franked payments in any accounting period exceed its franked investment income in the same period. If the franked payments exceed the franked investment income then ACT is payable on the excess plus the

ACT. Where the reverse is the position and there is an excess of franked investment income over franked payments in any accounting period, this is known as "surplus franked investment income". By s. 89 (3) of the Finance Act, 1972, the surplus is carried forward to the next accounting period and treated as franked investment income received in that period and so on. An alternative relief is available under s. 254 of the Act as substituted by s. 90 and Sched. 15 to the Finance Act, 1972. This provides that a company may require that the amount of the surplus shall, for certain purposes, be treated as if it were an equivalent amount of profit chargeable to corporation tax, thus reducing the amount of the surplus to be carried forward, as well as entitling the company to have paid to it the amount of the tax credit corresponding to the reduction of the surplus. The purposes for which franked investment income may be converted into profits chargeable to corporation tax in this way are:

(*a*) for setting off trading losses in the same or, broadly speaking, the preceding accounting period;

(*b*) deductions of charges on income;

(*c*) in the case of an investment company or life assurance company the deduction of management expenses, and

(*d*) for setting off against capital allowances.

By s. 255 of the Act, as substituted by Sched. 15, similar provisions apply to losses brought forward from previous years.

Just as under the old system a subsidiary could pay dividends to its parent without deducting tax as was then generally required, so it may now elect under s. 256 of the Act not to pay advance corporation tax, and the parent is then not entitled to the tax credit. Under certain conditions a trading company controlled by a consortium of other companies can also elect that s. 256 (1) shall apply. Dividends treated in this way are called "group income" and the section applies only to dividends and not to any other distributions. A relic of the old system of deduction of tax at source remains in the case of payments which are charges on the income of the company for corporation tax purposes such as interest, annuities and annual payments. These where paid by a subsidiary to its parent company may also be paid in full by election under s. 256.

The election under the section makes no difference to corporation tax which is still borne by the subsidiary, so that the parent does not have to pay corporation tax on group income any more than it does on franked investment income.

While companies are members of a group there is considerable freedom to make transfers of assets to each other without taxation consequences. Similarly, where one company in a group has paid advance corporation tax which cannot be set against its liability to corporation tax because it has no income to charge to the tax or where the ACT exceeds the liability to tax, the parent's ACT thus generated may be surrendered within the group to companies which have a liability for corporation tax in excess of any ACT credit of their own.

When the company's total liability to corporation tax is ascertained the ACT can be set off against so much of it as is charged on income. That which is charged on capital gains, being charged at a lower rate, is excluded from set-off.

It would be easy for a company to reap an advantage if in an accounting period it made distributions in excess of its profits, by utilising accumulated income reserves or when its income has been reduced for tax purposes by capital allowances. Section 85 (2) of the Finance Act, 1972, therefore restricts the right to set-off ACT to an amount equal to the amount of ACT which would have been payable in respect of a distribution made at the end of the accounting period which together with ACT would equal the company's income charged to corporation tax for that period.

If a company is acting as a trustee, so that it has no beneficial interest in its own profits, those profits are exempted from corporation tax by s. 243.

Corporation tax would be a simple subject if it were not for the idiosyncrasies of the close company, to which attention must now be turned.

CLOSE COMPANIES

When the shares of a company are held by the investing public, market pressures can be relied on to make sure that its affairs are conducted on commercial lines. But if a company is controlled by a small group of people, some of them directors as well as shareholders, the position is entirely different, because these people are free, in the absence of special legislation, to deal with the profits of the company in the way that will involve them in least tax.

Under the corporation tax system it is desirable, from the point of view of the Revenue, to restrict the amounts paid out to proprietors in a form which would otherwise reduce liability to corporation tax; it is even more desirable to prevent shareholders' liability to the higher rates of tax and investment income surcharge being reduced by unreasonable accumulations of net profits within the company. These somewhat conflicting aims are the inspiration of the rules about close companies contained in ss. 282 to 303.

Before one is able to speak fluently about close companies, the necessary vocabulary has to be acquired. The following are intended as explanations of the definitions given in the sections, reference to the actual wording being necessary whenever a particular case is to be tested.

Participator

The purpose of the definition is to combine, in the one concept of participator, not only all shareholders but also all loan creditors except banks. To prevent avoidance, it includes any other person who has, or can obtain or will be able to obtain, voting rights or an interest in the capital or income of the company. Some sections extend the definition to include a participator in another company that controls the company, but this is not part of the general definition.

Associate

For various purposes a participator or a director cannot stand alone, but must be judged by the company he keeps. His associates consist of:

(1) near relatives within the range of husband or wife, brother or sister, parent and upwards, child and downwards;

(2) partners;

(3) trustees of a settlement made by him or any of his near relatives (but not beneficiaries unless they come under one of the other heads);

(4) where he is interested (beneficially or not) in a trust or estate holding shares or obligations of the company, any other person so interested, except a mere beneficiary under a pension scheme.

Director

In addition to a director in the Companies Act sense, the definition covers any power behind the throne in accordance with whose instructions the directors are accustomed to act, and even a mere manager of the company's business, if he owns or controls, either by himself or with his associates, 20 per cent. or more of the ordinary shares.

To satisfy the last part of the test, the 20 per cent. may be owned or controlled wholly by the associates, without the "director" having any shares of his own at all.

Material interest

A person has a material interest in a company if he owns or controls, either by himself or with his associates, more than 5 per cent. of the ordinary shares, or if more than 5 per cent. of the distributable income could be apportioned to him, with or without his associates.

Again, it is sufficient if the 5 per cent. test is satisfied wholly by the associates.

Control

Control of a company means possession of, or the right to acquire, more than half of any of the following:

The share capital or issued share capital.

The voting power.

The income, if the whole of it were to be distributed to members.

The assets available for distribution among members in winding up.

In deciding how many people share control, any one

person is liable to have attributed to him the rights of his associates, the rights of his nominees, which presumably includes bare trustees, and the rights of any other company he controls, alone or with the help of associates. For example, if five unconnected men and their five wives each held 6 per cent. of the controlling shares, the company would be controlled by five people because each man would have attributed to him the rights of his wife-associate. If the five men were partners the five partners could be counted as one, or each partner could be counted as one with his wife, but he could not be counted as one with his partner's wife.

The definition of the close company itself can now be approached. A close company is one under the *control* either of five or fewer *participators* or of any number of participators who are also *directors*. A company is also a close company if, having begged the question and assumed that it was a close company, it is found that more than half the amount to be apportioned under the provisions considered on p. 70 could be eventually apportioned among five or fewer participators or participators who are directors.

A company not resident in the United Kingdom is excepted from the definition. With certain safeguards, a subsidiary of a non-close company is also excepted by a subsection that is particularly obscure unless it is kept in mind that one person or group may be in control under one branch of the definition of control at the same time as another person or group is in control under another branch of the definition. The exception applies to a company controlled by one or more non-close companies, always assuming that five other participators cannot be shown to be also in control and that the company is not a close company for any other reason, such as control by participators who are directors or because of the apportionment test. Shares held by an outside pension fund, but not the company's own fund, count as shares held by a non-close company.

There is another very important exception in favour of a company with 35 per cent. of its voting ordinary shares beneficially owned by the public, these shares having been dealt in and quoted on a recognised stock exchange in the United Kingdom, or a designated stock exchange elsewhere, within the previous twelve months. The "public" does not include a director or his associate, or an associated company, nor does it include any of the five "principal members" of the company, unless that member is a non-close company or an outside pension fund.

It is clear that practically every family company is a close company, including many with a stock exchange quotation.

THE TREATMENT OF CLOSE COMPANIES

The close company suffers from three main disabilities.

1. Extended Meaning of Distribution

By ss. 284 and 285 interest paid to certain categories of person counts as a distribution when paid by close companies, although it would not do so if paid by other companies. The disadvantages of a distribution, it will be recalled, are that it cannot be deducted in computing profits for corporation tax and gives rise at the time of payment to ACT, while on the other hand it may be charged to income tax under Schedule F and attract tax in the hands of the recipient at the higher rates as well as incurring investment income surcharge.

Annual payments other than interest and rent and royalties were also penalised when paid to a participator, but this has been abolished by the Finance Act, 1972.

However, interest is not a distribution unless the participator to whom (or to whose associate) it is paid is also a director and has a material interest. Even then interest up to 8 per cent. is allowed, but with the serious limitation that the total interest must not exceed 8 per cent. on the nominal amount of the issued share capital at the beginning of the accounting period. This restricts allowance of interest when the family has provided more finance by loan capital than by share capital, a very normal procedure.

The cost of providing benefits for a participator or his associate also ranks as a distribution, unless it is already taxed under Schedule E as a director's or employee's benefit (see p. 74).

2. Loans

Since a loan made by a company is not a distribution, a member could take a loan for an indefinite period as a method of extracting assets from a close company without paying income tax. Section 286 anticipates this manoeuvre by charging a close company with an amount equal to the ACT on any loan made to an individual participator or associate. This is not technically either corporation tax or ACT and so no tax credit accrues and it cannot be carried forward as surplus ACT.

For this purpose, a loan includes a debt left owing to the close company, for instance unpaid purchase money on the sale of an asset by the participator, but if the debt is incurred for supply of goods or services in the ordinary course of the company's business, the section does not apply unless the credit given exceeds six months. Under certain conditions a loan up to £15,000 is exempted if it is made to a full time director or employee of the company who does not have a material interest. By concession, tax on loans by trading companies to pay estate duty on their shares may be suspended for five years, where one third or more of the ordinary share capital is chargeable with the duty (see *British Tax Review* [1969], p. 441).

The loan is not automatically treated as income in the hands of the participator or associate, but if the company releases him from the loan the grossed up amount becomes his income at the date of the release under s. 287, and is liable to tax at the higher rates and the investment income surcharge on a sum equal to the loan accordingly. If, on the contrary, the loan is repaid the company can reclaim the tax originally charged. The result is that a loan can be used as a means of deferring tax at the high rates and the investment income surcharge but not ACT, on a disguised distribution. On the other hand it does not rank as a distribution for the purpose of the apportionment provisions considered below. A loan which is liable to tax under s. 451, as a capital sum paid to a settlor by a company connected with the settlement (p. 24), is not to be taxed again under s. 287.

The reference to an *individual* participator means that a close company can make a loan to another company which is its participator, without running into trouble under the section. The section probably applies to trustees, although in other contexts they are not considered to be individuals, and it also applies to participators who are companies not resident in the United Kingdom.

A loan for the purpose of a share incentive scheme is excepted from the effects of s. 286 by the Finance Act, 1973, s. 20, although there are provisions for bringing it into effect again if the loan ceases to be used in connection with the scheme.

3. Apportionment of Income of Close Companies

Withholding of company profits from distribution saves the members tax at the higher rates. Throughout the years under the different systems of company and personal taxation this difficulty has been dealt with by giving the Revenue authorities power in certain circumstances to treat the company's income as that of its shareholders. When corporation tax was introduced the earlier system of surtax directions was modified to suit the new tax by the introduction of the procedure of the "shortfall" assessment. Under the new system the mischief is dealt with by what is known as the "statutory apportionment of income", provision for which is laid down in Sched. 16 to the Finance Act, 1972. The Schedule introduces a completely new system of nomenclature to replace that which we had grown used to since 1965. No longer do we look for "shortfall" or "the required standard". Now para. 1(1) of Sched. 16 provides that the inspector may apportion the income of a close company among the participators. This can be done if the "relevant income" of the company for the accounting period exceeds its distributions, and the amount which may be apportioned is the amount of that excess. However, in the case of a trading company no apportionment will be made if the excess is not more than £1,000.

To find the relevant income, it is first necessary to calculate the distributable income. This means the profits for corporation tax, after deducting the corporation tax itself and eliminating any part of the profits due to capital gains. Although capital gains are charged to corporation tax, it is evidently not thought fair to compel a close company to distribute them. To these net profits there must then be added an amount equal to the qualifying distributions comprised in any franked investment income and group income, because these can reasonably be regarded as distributable income although not liable to corporation tax for reasons mentioned on p. 64.

At this stage a distinction has to be made between a trading company, as defined in para. 11 of Sched. 16, and an investment company. There is also a distinction between estate or trading income, which is more leniently treated because of the normal need to make reserves, and investment income where no such need generally exists; this part of the Schedule is unintelligible unless one remembers that a predominantly trading company may have some estate income or investment income, and a predominantly investment company may have some trading income.

To take first the case of a trading company:

(1) The relevant income will be so much of the distributable income as can be distributed without prejudice to the requirements of the company's business, including not only current requirements but those for the maintenance and development of its business. The onus appears to be on the Revenue to show that the relevant income could be distributed without prejudice to those requirements. Unless it can show this the relevant income for the purposes of the statutory apportionment is nil.

(2) In any case there is an overriding maximum for the relevant income equal to the whole of the distributable investment income (subject to a small abatement not exceeding £500) plus 50 per cent. of the estate or trading income.

(3) A trading company has a special privilege for small incomes. If the estate or trading income is less than £5,000 it is completely ignored, and if it is between £5,000 and £15,000 there is an abatement of one-half of the amount needed to make it up to £15,000. When the trading company is a member of a group, the figures of £5,000 and £15,000 have to be divided by the number of companies in the group, whether trading or investment companies, but excluding any that are completely dormant.

(4) A company which would otherwise be classed as an investment company is entitled to the same treatment as a trading company, if it exists to serve the purposes of a group of trading companies, whether as holding company or subsidiary. It is known as a *member of a trading group*. It cannot of course qualify for the abatement on small estate or trading incomes.

For an investment company:

(1) The relevant income is again the distributable income, less an amount which the company shows could not be distributed without prejudicing its business.

(2) Here, however, the argument is confined to any estate or trading income the company may have. Reserves of investment income cannot be justified by the requirements of the business.

(3) There is the same overall maximum of distributable investment income plus 50 per cent. of the estate or trading income.

If a close company whose income has been apportioned later distributes the apportioned income, any individual who has been taxed on it may have an equivalent proportion of the subsequent distribution excluded from his income for tax purposes.

Paragraph 18 of Sched. 16 provides a procedure for obtaining clearance from statutory apportionment of estate or trading income. After adoption of the accounts in general meeting, the company can send a copy to the inspector, who must make up his mind within three months of the application, or at the latest within three months of the furnishing of further particulars, whether or not he is going to proceed.

Consequence of Apportionment

When the inspector exercises his powers to apportion the income of a close company to its participators or sub-apportions them down the line through other companies to the eventual participators (as he has power to do), the sums so apportioned are treated as the income of the individual participator. The apportioned amount must be included in his income for tax purposes and is deemed to be the highest part of his total income.

It is likely, therefore, to be included in investment income for the purpose of the investment income surcharge if his total investment income, including the apportionment, amounts to more than £2,000. He cannot be assessed to the basic rate of income tax on his income thus apportioned so that it is only those who pay income tax at the higher rates or the investment income surcharge who will suffer by statutory apportionment. Although the liability of the participator to the basic rate of income tax is thus treated as discharged he cannot make an income tax repayment claim in respect of it. Any sum apportioned is treated for the purposes of ss. 52 and 53 as income not brought into charge to income tax, so that it cannot be used to support an annual payment made by the participator and entitle him to retain tax which he has deducted at source.

One small mitigation of the rigours of apportionment is granted by para. 5 (4) of Sched. 16, which provides that no individual shall be assessed to income tax by virtue of an apportionment unless the sum on which he is assessable amounts at least to £200 or 5 per cent., of the amount apportioned, whichever is the less.

Where the participator fails to pay the tax assessed on him as a result of an apportionment, a notice of liability to tax can be served on the company, which thereupon becomes liable to pay it. If the company does not pay within three months the Revenue may exercise their right of recovery from either the company or the participator.

In one case an apportionment may be made even where there is no excess of relevant income. This is where the company has been allowed a deduction for a charge on income, for example a covenanted payment to charity, which would not have been allowable for income tax at the higher rates or the investment income surcharge if it had been made by an individual. It does not apply where the annual payment consists of interest or is made wholly and exclusively for the purposes of the company's trade.

The Board of Inland Revenue have issued a very informative and comprehensive statement of practice with regard to the taxation of close companies which is set out in Appendix D.

SMALL COMPANIES

Section 95 of the Finance Act, 1972, created a third category of companies in addition to close and "non-close" ones. This is the "small company" which is taxed at a lower rate than the others. The word "small" refers not to its capital or assets but its profits in a particular accounting period and it qualifies for the lower rate if these are below £15,000. If the profits are between £15,000 and £25,000 there is a form of marginal relief. There are anti-avoidance provisions to prevent a business being carried on by a multitude of small associated companies, and for the purpose of the section a company is treated as the associated company of another if at a given time one of the two has control of the other or both are under the control of the same person or persons. The definition of control is a far-reaching one and companies which from a business point of view are wholly unrelated may well be associated. The old shortfall rules had a similar provision as to associated companies, and assurances were given by the Board that they would not be so rigorously enforced as to disqualify obviously unrelated companies from certain abatements then available. It is to be hoped that some similar concession will be made in the case of small companies.

DIRECTORS' BENEFITS

Expenses

It is sometimes thought that the formation of a company enables directors to obtain allowances for expenses to which they would not otherwise have been entitled. This is quite incorrect because the position of a director with regard to expenses is on the whole less favourable than that of a partner or proprietor of a business. By s. 195, any sum paid in respect of expenses by a company to a director, or an employee earning £2,000 a year or more including the expenses in question, is treated as the incomc of the director or employee and taxed in his hands under Schedule E. The director or employee is then left to claim any allowance to which he may be entitled under s. 189, and it is notorious that the Schedule E taxpayer is in a worse position than one assessed under Schedule D; a deduction is only allowed under Schedule E in respect of money necessarily incurred in travelling expenses or wholly, exclusively *and necessarily* incurred in other ways in the performance of the duties of the office, while the corresponding Schedule D rule in s. 130 merely stipulates that the amounts must be wholly and exclusively expended for the purposes of the trade.

By s. 196, benefits in kind provided by a company for a director or employee earning £2,000 per annum or more are treated in the same way. The basis of the charge on the director or employee is the expense incurred by the company, and not the value of the benefit. In *Wilkins* v. *Rogerson* [1961] Ch. 133 it was held that an employee earning less than £2,000 per annum could only be taxed on the second-hand value of a suit received by him as an emolument of his office, but this decision would not apply to a case covered by s. 196.

Section 196 (4) exempts the provision of meals in any canteen in which meals are provided for the staff generally, an exemption which is liberally applied to cover a directors' lunch room, so long as a canteen in the more ordinary sense is run in conjunction with it.

Living accommodation provided by a company for a director is always taxable as a benefit, however necessary it may be for business purposes (*McKie v. Warner* [1961] 1 W.L.R. 1230 and *Butter* v. *Bennett* [1962] Ch. 293). But the House of Lords in *Luke* v. *Commissioners of Inland Revenue* [1963] A.C. 557, showed that some limits must be placed on the operation of the section, when they decided that a director who paid a proper rent for a company house could not be taxed on the cost of certain outgoings and repairs borne by the company. Pennycuick, J., in *Westcott* v. *Bryan* [1969] 2 Ch., at p. 335, said that the decision in *Luke's* case should be confined to expenses for which a tenant would not ordinarily be responsible, so that a director could be assessed where the company paid for normal maintenance repairs to the house he occupied. It was also held in *Westcott* v. *Bryan,* and confirmed by the Court of Appeal [1969] 2 Ch. 324), that s. 196 permits the apportionment of expenses paid partly for business purposes and partly for the director's benefit, the apportionment to be made on the broad basis of what was fairly attributable to the use of the house as the taxpayer's home and what to the use of the house by the company; the apportionment should not be made by trying to count the number of days of each use.

In order to avoid the complication of assessing the director or employee and then dealing with his claim for deduction, it is possible for the company to agree with the inspector of taxes a list of proper expense allowances and benefits in kind, the agreed items being treated as expenses of the company in spite of ss. 195 and 196, but this is merely a matter of machinery and does not affect the principle laid down by the sections.

In cases where substantial allowances are made to directors and agreed for tax purposes, the justification is in all cases the nature of the business carried on and not the fact that it has been incorporated.

By s. 411 expenses of all business entertaining are disallowed except for overseas customers. The director, who can still have his own meal provided in a "staff canteen" without the expense being disallowed to the company, has perhaps come out of this restriction better than the partner. The partner's lunch room, formerly justified by the need to entertain, now has no claim to tax relief unless the overseas customers are sufficiently frequent.

Another method of rewarding a director or senior employee of a company is restricted by s. 186 and s. 78 of the Finance Act, 1972. Under the first section Schedule E tax can be charged on any gain realised by the *exercise* of a share option granted to him by the company. This reverses the rule in *Abbott* v. *Philbin* [1961] A.C. 352, where the House of Lords held that a share option granted to an employee was taxable only on its value at the time of the grant, which usually meant that it escaped taxation altogether because the value then was negligible. The effect of the section is now mitigated by ss. 78 and 79 of the Finance Act, 1972. The first of these sections excludes the operation of s. 186 from approved share option schemes which, within the rather narrow confines of Sched. 12 to the Act, are now once again allowed. After the legislation now contained in

s. 186 was introduced share options became ineffective for tax planning purposes and "share incentive schemes" whereby directors and executives were granted means of acquiring shares or interests in them through trust funds, special companies and so on were devised. As a counter-balance to the easing of the restriction on share options Parliament has now brought such schemes within the tax net by s. 79, unless they are, like share option schemes, approved by the Board. The rules for qualifying for approval are set out in Sched. 12 to the Act, and these are discussed in detail in chapter XII.

Pensions

It should also be remembered that, by s. 220 or (in the case of new schemes) s. 23 of the Finance Act, 1970, payments made by a company under a retirement benefits scheme in respect of directors or employees, whatever their salary level, are treated as part of the income of the director or employee; if the company does not pay premiums to provide the retirement benefits but carries the burden of the scheme itself, the director or employee is assessed on the notional amount which the company would have paid if it had arranged with an insurance company to secure the benefits.

Section 220 and s. 23 of the Finance Act, 1970, do not apply to an approved superannuation fund or certain other schemes approved by the Commissioners of Inland Revenue. Until 1973, no scheme could be approved which benefited a director in respect of his service during any period when he was a controlling director of the company. A controlling director is one who directly or indirectly controls more than 5 per cent. of the ordinary shares of a company which is itself controlled by the directors as a whole. This meant that the familiar "top hat scheme" could only be used if the director in question held 5 per cent. or less of the ordinary shares or, although the director in question owned more than 5 per cent., the company was controlled by people who were not directors. This restriction was removed by s. 15 of the Finance Act, 1973, and a controlling director is now almost in the same position as other directors. But not quite! It is understood that the Board will exercise some control where directors can fix their own salary levels and this will be done by means of the rules which they apply in granting approval of schemes. (see p. 149).

The result is that a controlling director is in exactly the same position with regard to pensions as a partner or sole proprietor of a business; if he wishes to make provision for his retirement, he must either rely on s. 226, which allows controlling directors, like professional men, to make certain payments for retirement annuities out of their net relevant earnings, or else he must claim the ordinary income tax relief against premiums paid on a life endowment policy (Chapter XVII, p.149).

Although s. 226 normally applies to controlling directors, there is an exception in the case of controlling directors of investment companies who are seldom the objects of Parliament's sympathy.

ESTATE DUTY

At one time the family company was frequently employed as a means of avoiding estate duty. As a result, sweeping provisions were enacted in the Finance Act, 1940, to ensure that business and other forms of wealth should bear roughly the same estate duty, whether the deceased held them in his own name, or controlled them through a company to which the Act applies. These provisions went further in some respects than was necessary to secure their purpose, and have been modified in favour of the taxpayer by the Finance Acts, 1954 and 1960.

The Finance Act, 1940, employs for estate duty purposes the definition of a company liable to surtax directions under s. 245 of the Income Tax Act, 1952, but extends it to companies incorporated outside the United Kingdom, while companies which are subsidiaries of exempted companies or in which the public are substantially interested are not excepted. Although s. 245 has been repealed, the definition contained in the 1952 Act is still used here, and it is necessary to recall that this refers to a company under the control of not more than five persons, any shareholders who are relatives, or partners, or nominees of each other or together interested in shares of the company held by a trust or estate, being counted as one.

The first method adopted by the Finance Act, 1940, for equating the position of a shareholder with a direct owner of assets is contained in s. 55. This section provides that shares which pass on death—and this includes shares which are deemed to pass under a gift *inter vivos* (*Sanderson* v. *Commissioners of Inland Revenue* [1956] A.C. 491)—are to be valued for estate duty not on the basis of their hypothetical open market value as shares but on the basis of the value of the company's net assets. Before the section can apply, it is necessary not only that the company should be a controlled company but also that the deceased himself should have had actual control by his voting power, or deemed control, within the seven years ending with his death. The cases in which control is deemed are now defined by s. 29 of the Finance Act, 1954. One case is where the deceased had control of the board for two continuous years within the seven, and because of this, articles of association are now usually drawn without any provision for a governing director. The second is entitlement to *more than half* of the dividends and debenture interest, which must also occur for two continuous years. The third is a beneficial interest in possession in *one half or more* of the shares and debentures, and this need not last for two years; if the deceased at any point of time within his last seven years held the shares and debentures, or a life interest in them, he is deemed to have had control unless somebody else had actual control of the company or the board at the same time. For this reason, an equal division of shares between two people without any casting vote, so far from preventing either having deemed control, may give it to both.

Shares held by the deceased as a trustee do not count towards control, unless he created the settlement himself. In *Barclays Bank, Ltd.* v. *Commissioners of Inland Revenue* [1961] A.C. 509 the deceased was the first named of four trustees holding shares of a family company, and it was argued that, although the deceased was the settlor, these shares could not be taken into account because he was bound to vote in accordance with the decision of the trustees as a whole. Since the House of Lords rejected this argument, a settlor of shares in a family company should be advised not to act as first-named trustee; whether he can safely act as trustee at all is an open question, as we saw on p. 28.

The assets to be valued under the Finance Act, 1940, include the goodwill of a trading company, an item which calls for skilful negotiation and sometimes for the assistance of a team of experts. Section 30 (1) of the Finance Act, 1954, did something to remedy the injustice which can arise when, in order to raise the estate duty, shares have to be sold at a price less than the valuation placed upon them. If the shares are sold at arm's length within three years after the death, a lower sale price can be substituted for the estate duty valuation. The Finance Act, 1973, s. 45, now takes this further in the case of quoted shares. If these are sold within twelve months after the date of death at less than the value on that date, the principal value of the aggregate of all such shares is reduced by the loss on the sale. Another important alleviation is contained in s. 66 of the Finance Act, 1960, which limits the value of assets to their use in the business, thus preventing an inflated valuation being placed on buildings which could only be realised by developing them for some quite different use. The reduction of 45 per cent. in the rate of duty on agricultural property and on industrial hereditaments, machinery and plant may also be available in the case of assets held by a company whose shares have to be valued under s. 55 of the Finance Act, 1940. The agricultural land, however, has to be occupied by the company for husbandry or forestry, which means that if tenanted agricultural property is transferred to a company the benefit of the reduced rate will always be lost. In valuing the assets, an appropriate allowance can be made for the possibility of a charge to tax on capital gains, but unless disposals in the near future are likely the allowance will only be small.

Shares of a class which has been dealt in on a United Kingdom stock exchange during the year ending with the death are exempt from s. 55, and this covers the majority of holdings in public companies, even if they are controlled by not more than five persons.

The second weapon is s. 46 of the Finance Act, 1940, which

enables the Inland Revenue to make a charge for estate duty on a company itself in certain cases where matters have been so arranged that no assets pass on a death. For this section to apply, it is necessary for the deceased to have made to a controlled company *at any time* a transfer of property or a payment of money, including a subscription for shares, and for him to have received benefits from the company during the seven years immediately before his death. If these conditions apply, the assets of the company itself can be charged with estate duty on his death in the proportion which the benefits received by the deceased bore to the company's income during the seven years. Section 88 of the Finance Act, 1965, contains special rules for computing the company's income for this purpose. Section 46 of the 1940 Act is not often invoked in practice but it has to be kept constantly in mind because its mere existence discourages, as it was meant to do, nearly all the schemes by which a man might take the benefit of the company's income without holding any shares to attract duty on his death. Remuneration for services is not counted as a benefit if it is reasonable, and if the head of the family takes a service agreement from his company after he has parted with his shares, it is essential to make sure that the remuneration can be justified.

When a controlling interest in a family company is sold, it is the custom for the vendors to give indemnities against any liability of the company for estate duty under this section. Although there is no statutory clearance procedure, the Estate Duty Office is prepared to give a limited clearance to a person required to enter into an indemnity in certain circumstances, including a sale at arm's length of shares which carry voting control of the company. Details of the procedure for obtaining clearance are given in the *Law Society's Gazette,* March, 1965, p. 183 and in *Taxation,* 10th January, 1965, p. 324.

It is not necessary to go into further details with regard to these estate duty provisions, because for the purposes of this book the main point is that estate duty will not generally be saved by transferring assets to a company in exchange for controlling shares. The person concerned will have to go further and deal with the shares of the company by settlement or gift if estate duty on his death is to be substantially reduced, but at least it can be said that shares of a company are easier to settle or transfer than the assets which they represent.

When a settlor has reduced his dutiable holding to a minority interest in the company, the open market valuation of his shares for estate duty is likely to be less than the proportionate value of the company's assets. How much less, involves the difficult problem of the hypothetical sale between an imaginary willing vendor and a non-existent willing purchaser. It has to be assumed that the sale could take place, in spite of restrictions in the articles of association on transfer of the shares, but the restrictions are not irrelevant, because it must be recognised that the purchaser would be bound by them in the future (*Re Crossman* [1936] 1 All E.R. 762). In *Re Lynall* [1971] 3 W.L.R. 759 the question was what information about the company's history and prospects should be assumed to be in the purchaser's possession. The Court of Appeal decided that, at any rate with a substantial block of shares, account must be taken of the replies a board of directors would, in practice, make to the reasonable questions in confidence of a purchaser's advisers. This was reversed in the House of Lords who held that an open market valuation of unquoted shares must be made without regard to confidential information in the possession of the directors since in practice the information would be available only to selected purchasers who would not constitute an "open market".

Section 51 of the Finance Act, 1973, changed the law again. It declares that for the purpose of determining the market value of unquoted shares it must be assumed that there is available to any prospective purchaser all the information which a prudent prospective purchaser might reasonably require if he was proposing to buy from a willing vendor by private treaty at arm's length. Whether the assumption embraces all the detailed information required by investigating accountants when a company is being taken over or a finance house is investing in it remains to be seen. The section applies in the case of deaths on or after 6th July, 1973.

Before arguing for too low a figure, when private company shares are being valued for estate duty or stamp duty, the repercussions on capital gains tax should be considered. A low valuation may be used as an argument against another shareholder who is trying to establish a high base value at 6th April, 1965, although in valuing minority interests much depends on the size of the holding. Since each holding has its own value, the price per share for a 5 per cent. holding may be no guide to the value of a 40 per cent. holding. The value for estate duty can also affect the capital gains position of the estate itself. Bearing in mind that gains accrued before the date of death are generally exempt, while the agreed value will form the base for gains realised in the future by the executors or the beneficiaries, an estate bearing a low rate of estate duty may occasionally profit from a higher valuation. For these reasons, the Share Valuation Department of the Estate Duty Office and the taxpayer's representatives sometimes find themselves using the arguments they learned from each other in the days before capital gains tax was invented.

CAPITAL GAINS TAX—VALUATION OF UNQUOTED SECURITIES

Section 51 of the Finance Act, 1973, also applies to the valuation of unquoted shares for capital gains tax purposes, and Sched. 20 to the Act contains rules for adjusting the base value accordingly. This may help the taxpayer when it is desired to establish as high a value as possible at 6th April, 1965. The section applies to a disposal after 6th July, 1973, but where this took place before that date and the amount of the gain or loss has not been finally determined there is some relief for the taxpayer. By para. 7 of the Schedule the actual date of the disposal is substituted for 6th July, 1973, if to do so will result in a smaller gain or greater loss.

Where there has been a part disposal before 6th July, 1973, the whole of the apportionment then made is recalculated in accordance with s. 51 in order to find the new base value of the remainder, but no recalculation of the earlier gain or loss, if finally determined, is permissible.

UNLIMITED COMPANIES

Disclosure is the price of incorporation for all limited companies. If it is desired to avoid filing accounts, advantage has to be taken of the exemption given by s. 47 of the Companies Act, 1967, to an unlimited company which has no parent–child relationship with a limited company. This is made easier by the provision in s. 43 for changing an existing limited company into an unlimited one.

To make the change, an application has to be lodged at the Companies Registry, with a form of assent signed by all the members, a statutory declaration by the directors and a print of the memorandum and articles in their new form. The fee is £5.

Whenever limited liability is not essential, it is worth considering the formation of a family company as an unlimited one, or the conversion of an existing company under the simple procedure of s. 43. This may not be possible where shares are held by trustees because the trustees will usually want the protection of limited liability.

Although s. 44 provides a similar method for unlimited companies to switch to limited liability, neither kind of company is allowed to change its sex more than once.

CHAPTER IX

TRADING COMPANIES

THE decision to form a trading company is usually taken for reasons not connected with taxation, the principal one being the advantage of limited liability, but in a doubtful case the effect of tax may be the determining factor.

So far as trading income is concerned, the scheme of company taxation discussed in Chapter VIII gives certain opportunities for tax saving. The company pays corporation tax on the whole of its income. We will assume that it is a close company, and this means that distributions may have to be made to avoid statutory apportionment, but need never exceed 50 per cent. of the trading income after paying corporation tax. In many cases, particularly in the early years, it will be possible for a company with proper accountancy advice to show, on the grounds described in Appendix D, that its relevant income is little or nothing. The promoters will be liable to income tax on their remuneration and possibly the investment income surcharge also on distributions.

The decision will usually depend on the answer to three questions:

> Are the proprietors going to be liable to heavy taxation at the higher rates?
>
> Will it be possible, under the apportionment rules, to reduce their higher rates of tax by making substantial reserves if the business is carried on by a company?
>
> If so, can these reserves be usefully employed in the business?

If the answer to any of these questions is No, then a company may not be advantageous, but in any case an estimate should be made of the combined taxes on a company, its shareholders and directors, as compared with taxes which would be borne by a sole trader or by partners.

In making the comparison it is useful to look at the company's income as though it consisted of three layers. The first is the layer paid out as directors' remuneration, which simply bears the personal income tax of the directors without the investment income surcharge. The second is the layer that may have to be distributed as dividends; this is the most highly taxed of all because it bears corporation tax and possibly income tax at the higher rates and the investment income surcharge, on what is left. Finally there is the layer that the apportionment rules permit the company to retain, liable only to corporation tax but locked up inside the company and not available for personal use of the shareholders without possibly suffering further tax.

If incorporation is justified by a calculation made on these lines, there are many points about the conduct of the company's affairs that must be watched.

First of all there are the special close company rules mentioned in Chapter VIII. The company should not be financed by loans *from* a participator with a material interest, who is also a director, or from his associate, without considering the limits beyond which interest on the loans will count as a distribution and not be deductible for corporation tax. The company should not in the ordinary way make loans *to* a participator or associate, because these will give rise to ACT, although if a company has been allowed to make a capital gain it may be better to extract it by way of loan, which will not attract income tax until it has been released or written off, than to pay it out as dividend.

The question of capital gains is even more important. A company carrying on a trade has the same right as an individual to what is colloquially known as a "roll-over" on replacement of business assets. The effect of s. 33 of the Finance Act, 1965, is to allow payment of corporation tax or capital gains tax, as the case may be, to be postponed when a business asset is sold at a gain, provided the proceeds are used to buy new assets within the classes listed below for use in the same business. This is done by ignoring the gain on the sale of the old asset and deducting the same amount from the acquisition cost of the new. The process can be indefinitely repeated and, although the day of reckoning will ultimately come when an asset is sold without replacement, the section enables the capital of the business to be kept intact for considerable periods.

Careful timing used to be needed to obtain the benefit of the section because the new asset had to be acquired within twelve months before or twelve months after the date of disposal of the old, unless these periods were extended by the Board. The position has now been eased by s. 37 of the Finance Act, 1973, which extends the period to three years after the disposal where the acquisition of the new asset takes place on or after 6th April, 1973, even if the sale of the old one took place before that date. The one year limit before the disposal remains so that there is a four year "spread".

Business assets to which the roll-over applies are divided into five classes:

(1) Land and buildings (except the stock-in-trade of a dealer in land or a developer) and fixed plant and machinery.

(2) Ships.

(3) Aircraft.

(4) Goodwill.

(5) Hovercraft.

If the acquisition of the new asset takes place on or after 20th April, 1971, it is not necessary for the replacement to be by an asset of the same class (s. 60 of the Finance Act, 1971). The operation of the roll-over is limited where the replacement asset is within the definition of a wasting asset.

Apart from assets to which s. 33 of the Finance Act, 1965, applies, the trading company should not be allowed to hold any capital assets which are likely to appreciate in value. Not only do capital gains made by a company bear corporation tax at the special rate, but the balance remaining after corporation tax will ultimately be taxed again in the hands of the members (pp. 92–93).

Although the former restrictions on remuneration of directors of close companies have been removed, the remuneration must still pass the general test of s. 130 as expenditure incurred wholly and exclusively for the purposes of the trade. It is not difficult to justify remuneration for working directors under this section, because trading profits do not earn themselves, but if any remuneration should be disallowed it would not be counted as a distribution for the purpose of statutory apportionment.

Practical Advantages

The formation of a company may also assist to a smaller extent in distributing the income among different members of a family. If a business man wishes to pay a small salary to his wife in order to obtain the additional personal allowances attracted by married women's earned income or the benefit of separate taxation of wife's earnings, it is simpler to make her a director of a company than to employ her in an unincorporated business. A reasonable director's fee to a wife or grown-up son or daughter can hardly be challenged even if the duties are slight, but in *Copeman* v. *William Flood & Sons, Ltd.* [1941] K.B. 202, the court doubted whether a substantial fee paid to a schoolgirl as director of a pig dealing company was allowable under s. 130 as money wholly and exclusively laid out or expended for the purposes of the trade.

In the same way, capital may be more easily distributed among the family when a company has been formed, because parcels of shares can be given away or settled without affecting the control of the business more than is desired.

Tax Loss Companies

A company which has sustained heavy and consistent losses may be more valuable than one which has made small profits, and advertisements for the sale of companies with losses are often seen in the press. Although these losses can in certain circumstances be used to save tax on profits in the future, the operation is not so simple as some people assume.

Section 177 (1) gives a trading company the right to carry forward losses against trading income assessed to corporation tax for succeeding accounting periods without limit. The difficulty is that this subsection relates to the income of one trade and, if a trading company has agreed losses, these can only be used to reduce future income of the same trade. It is essential that a tax loss company should not be purchased without making sure, first, that the company's trade has not been discontinued, and secondly that under the control of the purchaser the company will be able to continue the same trade and make profits from it. This means that the purchaser must be in a position to divert profitable business to the company in the way of its previous trade, and nothing can be gained by arranging for the company to take over another trade which, so far as the company is concerned, is a new one.

The right under s. 177 (2) to set off a trading loss against profits of any description (including capital gains) applies only to profits of the same or the preceding accounting period.

The difficulties are illustrated by the decision in *J. & G. Ingram & Son, Ltd.* v. *Callaghan* [1969] 1 W.L.R. 456, where a trade of manufacturing and selling rubber goods had been carried on for many years. Following a nine-months break, the company was taken over by new shareholders and resumed manufacture and sale of similar articles in plastic instead of rubber. The Court of Appeal affirmed the conclusion of the Special Commissioners that a new trade had been set up.

The obtaining of loss relief is further restricted by s. 483. No relief can be given, under either subs. (1) or subs. (2) of s. 177, if within three years before or after a change in ownership there was also a major change in the nature or conduct of the trade, or if a change of ownership took place at any time after the scale of the activities of the trade had become small or negligible and before any considerable revival. The effect of these restrictions is that many cases which might have been on the borderline under s. 177 will be decided in favour of the Revenue.

In the case of many tax-loss companies the money which has been lost is represented by debts due to its financial backers or its bank. These must be acquired as well as the company, since otherwise the new management's efforts to inject business will only benefit the creditors. It is best for the agreed consideration for the company as a tax loss to be allocated to the purchase of the debts since the satisfaction of a debt is treated for capital gains tax purposes as a disposal by a creditor who has purchased the debt, so the purchasers will want as high a base cost as possible. Nor will any capital loss arise on a disposal of debts, by the original creditors, so the vendors will prefer to get what they can for the debts and take their capital losses on the shares.

Sometimes debts are capitalised by the issue of shares which are sold. This may be convenient for the purchasers but will make no difference to the vendors since their base cost will be the value of the debts. This is usually negligible. It sometimes happens, however, that loans are made with the intention of capitalising them at some convenient time and owing to the losses this becomes impracticable. In such a case the original value of the debts may be the true consideration for the issue of shares and thus the base cost to the vendors (see *Cleveleys Investment Trust Co.* v. *C.I.R.* [1971], 47 T.C. 300). To secure this it is necessary that there should have been a binding agreement to capitalise the loans and as a precaution, anyone lending money to a speculative company should have such an agreement.

Section 101 of the Finance Act, 1972, contains anti-avoidance provisions almost identical with those in s. 483 which are aimed at the purchase of companies to obtain the benefit of their surplus ACT.

Transfer of Existing Business to Company

When a sole trader or a partnership transfers an existing business to a company, there is a discontinuance of the old business for tax purposes and a commencement of a new one. In spite of this, if the transfer is in consideration solely or mainly of the allotment of shares in the company, s. 172 allows losses of the old business to be carried forward against income received from the company by the former proprietors, relief being given in the first place against earned income.

A corresponding privilege for capital gains tax is given by para. 15 of Sched. 19 to the Finance Act, 1969. If a business is transferred as a going concern to a company by a person who is not a company, any capital gain the transferor would otherwise make on the business is carried forward and deducted from the base value of the shares. For this treatment to apply the whole of the assets of the business must be transferred, except that the transferor can retain the cash if he wishes. On the other hand the consideration for the transfer need not consist wholly of shares of the company, but if the transferor receives anything apart from shares he is, to that extent, liable to capital gains tax on his disposal of the business. In practice, the assumption of liabilities by the transferee is not treated as consideration for this purpose.

The carry forward under para. 15 means that the benefit of the capital gains tax exemption on death need not be lost by transferring a business to a company. Nor need the retirement exemption be affected, so long as the provisions of s. 34 of the Finance Act, 1965, are studied. An individual who gives away or sells, after reaching the age of sixty, the assets of a business he has owned for ten years is entitled to relief on capital gains up to a maximum of £10,000. A similar relief is given in respect of the shares in a family company which has been carrying on a trade during the ten years ending with the disposal of the shares (p. 46). When an individual's business has been transferred to a company in exchange for shares, the ten-year period can be made up by adding the period of ownership of the shares. On a strict reading of the section it might not apply to the retirement of an individual carrying on business in partnership, although it is understood that the Revenue consider the transfer of the whole or part of a partnership share to be covered.

CHAPTER X

PRIVATE INVESTMENT COMPANIES

WHILE the trading company, carefully handled, is a useful instrument of tax planning, the same is not true of the private investment company. There are very few cases where the formation of a company to hold the family investments can be justified on taxation grounds.

Special privileges are given to investment trusts, as defined in s. 359, but these are Stock Exchange companies which have to fulfil conditions beyond the reach of the ordinary family company. It will be assumed that the investment companies dealt with in this chapter not only fail to qualify as investment trusts but also fall within the close company definition.

The first possible advantage from the holding of properties by an investment company is the opportunity for making some reserves of income free of income tax, because the relevant income for purposes of statutory apportionment cannot, in the case of estate income, exceed 50 per cent. of what is left after paying corporation tax and may be a good deal less if the requirements of the business justify greater retentions. In most cases this advantage will be more than counter-balanced by the element of double taxation affecting all capital gains made by companies. Properties tend to grow in value, but their growth will be less fruitful in the sunless air of company ownership.

The reason for this is the joint effect of corporation tax and capital gains tax, even with the new system of a lower rate of tax for chargeable gains and tax credits. When a property is sold by a company, any gain will at once be liable to corporation tax, with no relief corresponding to the individual's right under s. 21 of the Finance Act, 1965, to have a year's gains, less half the first £5,000, charged to income tax instead. This is only the first stage. Whatever the lower rate of corporation tax proves to be the remainder of the capital gain falls into the company's coffers, with a resulting increase in the value of the shares. If the shares are disposed of, whether by sale or gift, there will be capital gains tax to pay at 30 per cent., subject to any relief available, on the proportion of the company's gain reflected in the value of the shares. Nor can this second liability be escaped by taking the remains of the gain out of the company. Capital dividends are treated exactly like other dividends. They rank as distributions, liable to income tax at the higher rates under Schedule F as well as investment income surcharge when received by the shareholder. The tax credit will go far to mitigate the double taxation effect but only at the lower rates. If the remains of the gain are left in the company until it is liquidated, it is true that payments made in respect of share capital in a winding up are not treated as distributions, but on the other hand the shareholders are back into capital gains tax, which is chargeable on all amounts received from the liquidator in excess of the base value of the shares.

It is clear that property likely to appreciate in value is better held by an individual than by a company. On the other hand there may be a case for a company to hold wasting assets, like short leaseholds. In the case of wasting assets, Scheds. 6 and 8 to the Finance Act, 1965, contain complicated provisions for reducing the allowable expenditure, so that a sale of a short leasehold at less than cost can still throw up a capital gain, but these rules do not apply to the shares of a company holding wasting assets even though the shares will tend to depreciate with the underlying assets.

The second advantage in holding properties through properly constituted investment companies is that they may find it easier than an individual, especially if the individual is already classed as a dealer, to show that realisations are changes of investment rather than evidence of dealing in land. This advantage is limited by the wide provisions in s. 488 for taxing under Case VI of Sched. D gains of a capital nature obtained from artificial transactions in land. The distinction between investment companies and dealing companies is important mainly in connection with the calculation of relevant income for statutory apportionment of income, where an investment company has the privilege that capital gains are not included in distributable income, and the penalty that the relevant investment income cannot be reduced by showing that reserves are needed for the maintenance and development of its business.

Management Expenses

The third main reason for transferring properties to an investment company is the chance to convert unearned income into earned income. Although the distinction between earned and unearned income has in theory disappeared under the new unified system of personal taxation the surcharge on investment income over £2,000 still preserves it to some extent. Thus if income from the company can be received otherwise than by a distribution the surcharge may be avoided.

The way in which an investment company can convert what would otherwise be investment income into earned income is by paying it out as directors' fees or remuneration. This procedure, so far from saving any tax, would be liable to increase the total tax payable unless sums disbursed by the company to its directors were allowed in the company's own tax computations as a charge against the company's income. This can be achieved by relying on s. 304, which enables an investment company to deduct any sums disbursed as expenses of management in computing its profits for corporation tax. In other words, a company holding property can set off against its taxable income the expenses of managing the company, a privilege without parallel in the case of an individual property owner, and these expenses may include directors' fees and remuneration.

In addition, s. 306 allows an investment company to claim capital allowances for machinery or plant used for the management of its business, as though it were carrying on a trade.

Unfortunately the scope of s. 304 has been severely limited by the courts. It is possible to take two views of the way in which the section should operate. The typical taxpayer's view is that relief should be given for all sums which the company *bona fide* disburses; since there is no condition similar to the famous "wholly and exclusively" in s. 130 relating to expenses under

Case I of Schedule D, it is not open to the Revenue to enquire into the merits of any payment which the company, in its wisdom, sees fit to make. The contrary view would be that it is a question of fact in each case whether the sums voted by the company are truly "expenses of management" within the meaning of the section. These briefly, were the arguments put forward in the case of *L. G. Berry Investments, Ltd.* v. *Attwooll* [1964] 1 W.L.R. 693.

L. G. Berry Investments, Ltd., had an issued capital of £40, held between three members of the same family who were also the directors. The company was financed by interest-free loans from the same people, and its business was to advance money on mortgage. The gross income for the year in question was £1,800 1s. 4d., from which £600 was credited as a fee to each of the three directors, leaving a net surplus of 1s. 4d.

The affairs of the company were carried on with a reasonable amount of formality. It had no office of its own, but the books and seal were kept at the flat of one of the directors, together with a cash book and paying-in book from which the accountant wrote up the books. Seven directors' meetings were held during the year and at least one of the directors inspected all properties offered as security, the mortgagors being introduced by the company's solicitor.

In these circumstances, the special commissioners decided that it would not be in accord with reality to call the £1,800 expenses of management, and they granted relief only in respect of £200 for each director, a total of £600. In the High Court, Plowman, J., refused to disturb their decision.

It should be remembered that in all tax cases the High Court finds only on points of law. In the present case the decision of Plowman, J., was, first, that it is always a question of fact whether directors' remuneration, properly voted under a company's articles of association, is "expenses of management" and, secondly, that the commissioners had evidence on which they could come to the conclusion that £600 was the proper total for the *Berry* company to pay. But although the figure of £200 per director was not strictly part of the High Court decision, there is no doubt it tends to be taken as a yardstick in comparable cases.

The moral of the decision (if morals have anything to do with it) is that the draft accounts of an investment company should, if possible, be agreed with the inspector before the remuneration is voted. Although inspectors will usually accept a waiver by a director of remuneration voted to him, but subsequently disallowed under the section, at any rate where it has not actually been paid, it seems clear that in law the remuneration becomes his income when it is credited to him in the accounts, and the inspector could insist on taxing it in the director's hands.

In the *Berry* case, there was evidence that the £1,800 had been voted in pursuance of a policy that substantially the whole of the company's income should be disposed of in this way. It is advisable to make it clear that the quantum of directors' fees is related to the value of the directors' services rather than to the amount of the company's income. And it is better to leave more than 7p in the kitty.

No credit can be taken against a statutory apportionment of income for remuneration paid but disallowed under s. 304.

Properties Contrasted with Securities

The position of an investment company holding property can be summarised as follows. The principal remaining advantages are the accumulation of a certain amount of estate income free of tax at the higher rates and the conversion of some income into earned income. The second can only be marginal in most cases since the decision in *L. G. Berry Investments, Ltd.* v. *Attwooll.* In the other side of the scale must be weighed the severe penalty of double taxation on realisation of capital gains by the company, and the fact that the income of the company, not being franked investment income, is subject to corporation tax.

An investment company holding securities is in an even worse plight. The relevant income for distribution is 100 per cent. of the investment income. The decision in the *Berry* case bears even more hardly on the management expenses claim, since it is difficult to justify substantial remuneration for directors who only have to look after a portfolio of shares. On top of this there is the element of liability to double taxation whenever the company realises an investment at a gain. The only comparatively bright spot is the exemption of franked investment income from corporation tax.

If this gloomy picture of company taxation suggests that something ought to be done about an existing company, it is necessary to remember that s. 460 provides for the cancellation of tax advantages from certain transactions in securities. A reconstruction designed to extract assets, whether from a trading company or an investment company, may be a transaction in securities within the meaning of the section. Section 464 contains a procedure for applying to the Board of Inland Revenue for clearance, which it will usually be wise to operate.

The liquidation of a company can be counted as one of the transactions, the combined effect of which leads to the tax advantage. Until recently it was thought that a liquidation by itself did not constitute a transaction in securities, so that the simple remedy of winding up the company altogether, as distinct from reconstructing, would not generally be caught by s. 460. This is now in some doubt as the result of *Commissioners of Inland Revenue* v. *Joiner* [1973] S.T.C. 224. However, in that case there were special circumstances as the liquidation resulted from an agreement between the taxpayer and minority shareholders and it was held by Goulding, J., in the Chancery Division that the tax advantage which arose from the liquidation was a consequence of the agreement which was a transaction in securities as defined in s. 467.

In the case of companies under the control of not more than five persons, and unquoted companies generally, the section is particularly drastic. It is apt to catch any consideration received in non-taxable form out of assets which the company could have distributed as dividend if it had gone about matters differently. In *Commissioners of Inland Revenue* v. *Cleary* [1967] 2 W.L.R. 1271, where two sisters sold their shares in one company to another company which they also controlled, it was held by the House of Lords that this method of extracting funds from the second company was caught by the section, since the second company could have used the money to declare a dividend instead.

Money which a company has borrowed from the bank may

nevertheless be available for distribution by way of dividend in this sense, with the result that a tax advantage is obtained if the money is used to buy from a member some shares which he holds in another company. This was decided in *Commissioners of Inland Revenue* v. *Brown* [1971] B.T.R. 857, a decision which also shows the limits of the defence that the transaction or transactions were carried out for *bona fide* commercial reasons and that none of them had as their main object, or one of their main objects, to enable tax advantages to be obtained.

CHAPTER XI

COMPANIES FORMED FOR SPECIAL PURPOSES

SERVICE COMPANIES

PROFESSIONAL men who could save tax by incorporation may, by etiquette or by law, be denied this remedy.

A partial solution to the problem has been sought in the formation of a service company, which supplies the professional firm under contract with its material needs, in the way of premises, staff and equipment, while the firm continues to carry out its professional duties. The firm pays the company a fee, which reduces the partners' tax, at the same time enabling the company to make a profit which it puts to reserve.

The amount of tax which can be saved in this way is limited by three considerations.

In the first place the firm will not be allowed to pay away the whole, or anything like the whole, of its profits to the service company, and this is the principal limitation on the scope of the operation. The reason is that s. 130 specifically prohibits deduction from profits of any amounts not wholly and exclusively laid out or expended for the purposes of the business; if the firm pays out more for service than can be justified, allowing a reasonable profit to the company, then the payment will be disallowed for tax in the firm's own accounts. In practice the payment to be made is a matter for negotiation with the inspector of taxes.

Secondly, if a firm for its own reasons makes an additional payment to the company in one year with a corresponding reduction in later years, the extra may be disallowed on the ground that it is not a proper expense of the year of payment. This was decided in *Stephenson* v. *Payne, Stone, Fraser & Co.* [1968] 1 W.L.R. 858, a case which in other respects vindicated the use of a service company by a firm of chartered accountants.

Thirdly, the company, as a close company, must distribute its profits up to the amount of its relevant income for the purposes of statutory apportionment. The income derived from the firm will be trading income with a required standard of not more than 50 per cent, and it will be difficult to justify less when the requirements of the business are directed mainly to tax saving.

The reserves made by a service company can be used to provide working capital for the firm, to buy new assets and to pay pensions to retiring partners. The company is usually unlimited because limited liability is of no advantage, but the right of an unlimited company to buy its own shares enables the shares held by a partner retiring from the firm to be returned to the common pool without difficulty, and later re-issued when new partners come in.

Service companies have been formed occasionally by solicitors, and perhaps more often by accountants and stockbrokers. It is doubtful whether the trouble and expense of running a service company can be justified except in the case of very large firms, although it may have attractions for the prosperous one-man practice, where the problem of reconciling the interests of partners with differing income levels does not arise.

A special type of service company may help a solicitors' practice to avoid the problems of partial exemption under VAT. If the exempt supplies, such as insurance broking, mortgage broking and sub-letting of business premises are made by the company, the practice can be confined to taxable supplies, so that full credit is available under s. 3 of the Finance Act, 1972, for VAT suffered on inputs.

"FILM STAR COMPANIES"

The principles of this type of company also interest writers and cricketers, and anyone who relies for a living on exploiting his talents.

The film star company operates by securing the services of the star under a service agreement, and then entering into contracts with producers to make the services of the star available. The main object is to save tax by accumulating reserves within the company, and in principle it is affected by the same considerations as any close company carrying on a trade. The difference is mainly one of degree, because the higher rates of tax fall with exceptional severity on film stars and other personalities liable to wide fluctuations of income. These fluctuations can be ironed out if the company pays a level salary in bad years as well as good, and if it were proved that surplus income of a good year was being retained to meet future commitments under the service agreement, it might be possible to secure a reduction in the relevant income under the statutory apportionment provisions. It was held in *Davies* v. *Braithwaite* (1933), 18 T.C. 198, that an actress was taxable on income from foreign engagements as part of her profession carried on in the United Kingdom. For this reason it is advisable for the star to form a separate non-resident company for foreign contracts.

The sale of shares in a company in order to convert income from personal activities into capital is restricted by s. 487.

CHAPTER XII

SHARE OPTION AND SHARE INCENTIVE SCHEMES

UNTIL 1966 companies frequently rewarded directors and senior employees by granting them options to buy shares. The theory was that, if by their efforts they improved the company's fortunes, they deserved to participate in the improved value of the equity. Sometimes the reason for such a scheme being introduced was that the directors and employees concerned had not the capital to buy their shares, or at least not sufficient capital to risk in them. What was perhaps a more important aspect of the matter in many directorial minds was that until 1965 there was no capital gains tax apart from the old Case VII tax on short term dealings.

In *Abbott* v. *Philbin* [1961] A.C. 352 the House of Lords held that a share option granted to an employee was taxable on its value at the time of the grant. This usually meant that it escaped taxation because normally share options were granted at the current price since the theory was that the director's effort would increase this over a period. In 1966 what is now s. 186 reversed this rule and provided that where a person realised a gain by the exercise, assignment or release of a right to acquire shares in a body corporate, obtained by him as a director or employee of that body corporate, he should be chargeable to tax under Schedule E. The amount chargeable under the section is an amount equal to his gain as computed in accordance with the rules laid down by the section. No tax is charged under the section on the grant of the option, but when it is exercised the gain is taken to be the difference between the amount which reasonably can be expected to be obtained from the sale of the shares in the open market and the amount or value of the consideration given either for the shares or for the grant of the option. The gain realised by the assignment or release or the option is taken to be the difference between the amount or value of the consideration for the assignment or release and the amount or value of the consideration given for the grant of the right.

The section applies only in the case of an option obtained by a person as a director or employee of a body corporate. It lays down that the option is treated as obtained by a person in that capacity (1) if it is granted to him by reason of his office or employment as a director or employee who is chargeable to tax in respect of that office or employment under Case I of Schedule E, or (2) if the right is assigned to him and was originally granted to someone else by reason of his office or employment. The section also applies where the rights have been granted to the director or employee after he has ceased to hold office, in which case the option is treated as granted in the last year in which he was employed. There are other anti-avoidance provisions in the section affecting arrangements between two or more persons holding options taxable under the section if the result of those transactions is that a person holding an option ceases to do so, and either he or a connected person acquires a similar right.

These far reaching provisions effectively removed from share option schemes all their tax advantages and in their place a variety of forms of share incentive schemes arose. All these schemes avoided granting options or rights to acquire shares and became schemes whereby shares could be directly acquired on favourable terms, or through special investment companies, or in some cases by the use of loans or deferment of payment of the purchase price. These escaped tax.

Following the passing of the Finance Act, 1972, tax advantages of share option schemes become available again in the case of "approved share option schemes" and by s. 79 share incentive schemes are brought within the tax net unless they are "approved share incentive schemes". In fact it is difficult to see why anyone should now bother to set up share incentive schemes when the simpler and more effective option scheme is once more allowed and similar rules apply to both.

Share Incentive Schemes

Section 79, as amended by s. 19 of the Finance Act, 1973, applies when a person acquires shares or an interest in shares in a body corporate in pursuance of a right conferred on him or an opportunity offered him as a director or employee of that or *any other* body corporate otherwise than in pursuance of a public offer. It will be seen that the shares affected need not be those of the company of which the person is a director or employee.

A person will not be taxed under the section if the acquisition is in pursuance of a scheme approved under Sched. 12 to the Act or under an employees' profit-sharing scheme and provided that certain conditions in the section are complied with.

Subject to certain safeguards for the Revenue, acquisitions of shares by directors and employees on normal terms are excluded from the effect of the section. Nevertheless, these provisions could react unfairly on shareholders in companies controlled by their directors and employees and the amendments made by the Finance Act, 1973, do something to alleviate their position.

Share Option Schemes

Section 78 of the Finance Act, 1972, exempts approved share option schemes from the effects of s. 186. There is one exception to this general exemption. Where the option has been obtained under an approved scheme but the aggregate of the consideration (if any) given by the recipient, and the price at which he is entitled to acquire the shares under the option, is less than the market value of other issued shares of the same class at the time he obtains the option, he is chargeable to tax under Schedule E in the year of assessment in which he obtains the option on the amount of the difference. This tax will be a deduction for capital gains tax purposes on the first disposal of the shares acquired under the option. Apart from this particular provision, capital gains tax applies in the ordinary way to disposals of shares acquired under an approved option scheme, the base value of the shares being the actual cost of acquisition, and not the market value, although the acquisition was not at arm's length. Approval must be granted by the Board if the conditions laid down in Sched. 12 to the Act are complied with. If this is the case, the Board has no discretion in the matter and approval is mandatory. If after approval is given any of the conditions in the Schedule cease to be satisfied, approval may be withdrawn, and if a company is aggrieved by the failure of the Board to approve the scheme or by the withdrawal of approval it may appeal to the Special Commissioners.

Conditions for Approval for Schemes

There are three types of conditions, all of which must be satisfied, and which apply respectively to the scheme, its participants and the shares concerned. Each must satisfy the various conditions. Some of the conditions apply to both share option and share incentive schemes, while others apply to one or the other type of scheme.

Conditions applicable to both types of scheme

(1) The scheme must have been adopted by the holders of the ordinary share capital of the company by ordinary resolution in general meeting.

(2) The option, or the shares in the case of the incentive scheme, must not be capable of being acquired under the scheme more than ten years after its adoption.

(3) The shares must be shares in the company of which the participants in the scheme are directors or employees or in a company controlling it. Where the employing company is owned by a consortium the shares may be shares in a member of that consortium provided that it beneficially owns not less than three-twentieths of the capital of the employing company.

(4) The shares must be either quoted on a recognised Stock Exchange or shares in a company which is not under the control of another company.

(5) The majority of shares of the same class must not be shares which were acquired under share option or share incentive schemes. There is a limitation on the amount of shares which may be issued under approved schemes. If the ordinary share capital does not exceed £2,000,000 the limit is 10 per cent. If it does exceed £2,000,000 the limit is 5 per cent. or £200,000 whichever is the greater.

(6) Only full-time directors or full-time employees of the company may be eligible to participate in the scheme. This might be unfair on a person working full-time as a director or employee of two or more companies within a group but not full-time for any one of them. Such a person will, in practice, be treated as eligible to participate in a scheme which is open to directors or employees of any of the companies for which he works. This concession applies not only to parents and subsidiaries but associated companies, by which is meant a company on whose board the group is represented because of the group's shareholding or other financial interest.

Conditions applicable to share option schemes only

(1) The maximum which a participant may invest under the scheme must not exceed four times his relevant emoluments for the year of acquisition or for the preceding year, whichever is the greater. "Relevant emoluments" are defined as such of the emoluments of the office or employment which qualifies him to participate in the scheme as are liable to deduction of tax under P.A.Y.E. after deducting expenses, allowances and benefits in kind. This limit applies to the aggregate of the options obtainable under the particular scheme or previous schemes approved under the schedule. Shares obtained under a share incentive scheme approved under the schedule are also aggregated for the purposes of this limitation. In calculating the amount of option available to "a group director or employee" who works for two or more companies under the concession mentioned above only his earnings from participating companies will be taken into account.

(2) Options under the scheme must not be capable of being exercised later than seven years after they are obtained, nor later than six months after the participant ceases to hold the office or employment which qualified him to participate in the scheme. However, the option may be exercised within twelve months of his death if he dies at a time when it was still capable of being exercised by him.

A concession in practice has been announced by the Board in the case of a participant who ceases to hold the office or employment on taking up another qualifying full-time post with the same company. Strictly his rights would have to lapse after six months, but the Revenue will not regard a cessation as having occurred so long as he works full time within the group as a director or employee of one or more companies, if at least one of those companies is a participating company. This practice thus also recognises the position which may obtain when a man is promoted so as to become a whole time working director or employee within the group, but sharing his time between various companies as envisaged in the concession mentioned above.

(3) Options must not be transferable.

(4) The option price must be stated at the time it is granted, and must not be "manifestly less" than the current market value of shares of the same class, but the scheme may provide for such variations in the stated price as may be necessary to take account of any variation in the share capital of the company issuing the shares. "Manifestly less" is a somewhat vague phrase and it remains to be seen what the authorities, and, if necessary, the courts, consider to be manifest. Obviously it would be wise to fix the price as close as possible to the current market price if that price itself cannot be the stated price.

(5) The shares to be issued under the option must not be subject to any special restrictions other than restrictions attaching to all shares of the same class.

Conditions which apply to share incentive schemes only

These correspond to those set out above which apply to option schemes, with the necessary variations and adjustments to meet the different type of scheme.

(1) There are the same maximum limits.

(2) There must be restrictions on transfers of the shares acquired under the scheme so long as any special restrictions under the scheme attach to them which do not attach to all shares of the same class.

(3) The minimum price at which shares may be acquired is subject to two restrictions. It must not be "manifestly less" than the current market value of the shares at the time of their acquisition. This obviously refers to the value of shares subject to special restrictions under the scheme because there is a further

requirement that the minimum price must not be less than 80 per cent. of the current market value of shares of the same class, which are not subject to such special restrictions. There are provisions making the minimum price applicable where only an interest in shares is obtained (for example under a trust) or where the price is payable by deferred payments.

There is also a protection for the participant who might be called upon to pay his deferred instalments or repay a loan at a time when the current market value of shares of the same class not subject to the scheme is less than the price at which his shares were acquired under the scheme. In such case the scheme may provide for an appropriate reduction of the minimum price.

(4) Any special restrictions under the scheme must cease not later than seven years after the acquisition of the shares.

(5) The scheme must provide that the same restrictions as apply under the scheme to the shares being acquired shall apply to any bonus shares issued in respect of them. On the other hand, where there is a rights issue the rights must be on the same terms as are available to the shareholders generally.

Conditions to be satisfied by the director or employee

A participant must retain beneficial ownership of his shares for a period of three years from the date of acquisition of his option under a share option scheme, or shares under a share incentive scheme. If, however, he ceases to be a director or employee by reason of injury, disability, dismissal for redundancy or death, the period comes to an end whether three years have elapsed or not. Where a company, as a result of a take-over, is entitled to acquire a participant's shares under s. 209 of the Companies Act, 1948, this compulsory acquisition will not be deemed to be failure to retain beneficial ownership for the required period.

If the shares are shares in a close company there is a familiar type of restriction which we have seen in connection with distributions (p. 68). Directors or employees who have a "material interest", as defined in s. 285, may not be participants in their company's scheme.

Consequences of Non-Approved Share Incentive Scheme

If a director or employee acquires shares by means of an unapproved share incentive scheme, subs. (4) applies and he will be charged to tax under Schedule E. The amount on which he will be charged will be the excess of the market value of the shares at the end of the period prescribed by the section over the market value at the time of acquisition. The period prescribed by subs. (6) is the period ending at the earliest of the following times:

(*a*) seven years from the acquisition;

(*b*) the time when the person concerned ceases to have a beneficial interest in the shares; and

(*c*) in the case where a person has acquired shares (as opposed to an interest in them), the time when the shares cease to be subject to any special restrictions other than those applying to the whole class.

It should be remembered that the tax is chargeable at the end of the period whether there has been a disposal or not.

Any benefit received by the holder of shares which is not enjoyed by the majority of ordinary shareholders is also taxable under the section. Amounts chargeable under the section are deemed to be earned income and the section does not apply to arrangements whereby employees receive as part of their emoluments shares as part of a profit-sharing scheme (subs. (8)). The tax chargeable is allowable as a deduction in calculating the chargeable gain on the first disposal of the shares.

A loophole in s. 79 was left when the Act was passed which the Chancellor of the Exchequer announced he would close in the 1973 Finance Bill retrospectively to 18th October, 1972. When shares acquired under a scheme are subject to restrictions which are imposed as a condition of a loan rather than the terms of issue or the trusts of a deed they escaped the effect of the section in its original form. The Chancellor gave an assurance that the legislation would not affect loans arranged independently of the scheme. These provisions are contained in the Finance Act, 1973, Sched. 8.

Not all schemes are introduced at a late stage of a company's development or specifically as share incentive schemes. Quite often a company is formed with a special class of shares which it is intended shall be taken up by directors and executives. They may nevertheless be schemes within the section if shares are acquired by a person as a result of "an opportunity offered to him as a director or employee". This is a widely-drawn provision and it behoves the tax adviser to look carefully at the capital structure of a company and warn of the perils of s. 79 where it seems likely to apply.

CHAPTER XIII

PARTNERSHIPS

THE estate duty and taxation rules described later in this chapter apply both to professional people, who operate partnerships because they must, and to businessmen who choose partnership as an alternative to a trading company or a private investment company for the reasons mentioned in Chapters IX and X. The use of insurance for some partnership problems is dealt with in Chapter XVII.

Before considering the treatment of partnerships, it must be pointed out that a partnership cannot exist except for the purpose of carrying on a business. Joint ownership of property does not of itself create a partnership, even if the profits from the property are shared (s. 2 of the Partnership Act, 1890). Because of this rule, it is sometimes doubted whether the holding of investments amounts to a partnership activity. It is the view of the authors that the holding and management of investments under modern conditions frequently constitutes a business appropriate to be carried on by partners, although the income from the investments would not be earned income; there is some support for this view in the way the statutes recognise the holding of investments as a business in the case of companies.

One great advantage of a partnership is the complete freedom of the partners can be carefully regulated by the partnership accumulated profits from the firm or to reduce capital. The rights of the partners can be carefully regulated by the partnership agreement which may be drawn on similar lines to the articles of association of a private limited company, with provision for meetings, voting rights and management by "directors".

From 6th April, 1972, the admission of a wife as an active member of a partnership may be a suitable method of providing her with earnings which can be separately taxed under s. 23 of the Finance Act, 1971.

By s. 155, a company which is in partnership with other people is subjected to corporation tax on its share of the profits, but individual partners remain liable to income tax and surtax.

Limited Partnerships

If some of the people engaged in the business really need limited liability, which might be the case with trustees of a discretionary trust, but the hazards of close company taxation are found to be unjustified in the particular circumstances, then the Limited Partnerships Act, 1907, might be considered. There is little experience of the working of this Act, which came into force at the very time when the introduction of private companies by the Companies Act, 1907, gave what was to prove a more satisfactory answer for the next fifty-eight years.

Any lawful business can be carried on by a limited partnership, which is cheaper to form and run than a company, the only formalities being registration of certain particulars with the Registrar of Companies and registration under the Business Names Act, 1916, in circumstances where an ordinary partnership would have to register. Indeed, the ordinary law of partnership applies except so far as it is modified by the 1907 Act or the express terms of the agreement.

The limited partner must contribute an amount of capital, stated in the particulars, which forms the ceiling for his liability to creditors of the firm. He cannot withdraw his capital during the continuance of the partnership, but this need cause no difficulty because the limited partnership can be at will and the limited partner can be given express power to serve a dissolution notice himself. In the absence of agreement, the death of a limited partner does not terminate the partnership and the firm can retain the deceased's capital which might sometimes be convenient. The share of a limited partner can be assigned without difficulty, and there is nothing to prevent him metamorphosing at any time into a general partner and vice versa. While a limited partner he takes no part in the management of the business, which means that his share of profits is not earned income.

The terms on which a limited partner is to share in profits of the firm can be tailored to requirement by the agreement in an almost endless variety of ways. He can be given the profits up to a certain figure, or over a certain figure, or it can be provided that he shares in income profits but not in capital gains.

ESTATE DUTY

There are three possible situations which may arise under the partnership agreement on the death of a partner:

(1) His share may pass to his executors as part of his estate, the surviving partners having no option to purchase it. In this case the share is liable to duty as property of which the deceased was competent to dispose under s. 2 (1) (*a*) of the Finance Act, 1894.

(2) His share may be subject to an option (granted otherwise than by his will) in favour of the surviving partners. Here there is a charge to estate duty under s. 2 (1) (*f*). If the option is exercised, the effect of s. 37 (5) of the Finance Act, 1969, is that the estate is liable to duty to the extent of the option price; the surviving partners are liable to duty on any value of the share in excess of the option price, unless they can claim exemption under s. 3 of the Finance Act, 1894, on the ground that the property passed by reason only of a *bona fide* purchase from the deceased for full consideration in money or money's worth paid to him for his own use and benefit. The option payment itself seems in practice to be counted as consideration, although it is paid to the executors and not the deceased. Moreover a partnership agreement containing mutual options on a commercial basis would probably constitute full consideration for this purpose (cf. *A.G.* v. *Ralli* (1936), 15 A.T.C. 523). If the option is not exercised, or the option price is not less than the value of the share, the estate is liable to duty on the full value of the share but no more.

(3) His share may vest automatically in the surviving partners. This brings into operation another head of charge under s. 2 (1) (*e*) which reads as follows:

"(*e*) without prejudice to section 3 of this Act, property consisting of an interest of the deceased as a partner under a partnership agreement, being an interest to which under the terms of that or some other agreement some person other than the deceased's executor as such becomes or will become entitled on or by reference to the deceased's death otherwise than by the exercise of an option to acquire that interest."

It will be noted that the exemption for purchase under s. 3 is preserved. The consideration required by the section may consist of the mutuality of the arrangements between the partners, or of an agreement by junior partners to give more time and attention to the affairs of the partnership than the deceased was bound to do. In the case of *A.G.* v. *Boden* [1912] 1 K.B. 539, it was held, even where the partners were a father and his two sons, that an agreement of this sort was full consideration for the share of goodwill passing to the sons on the father's death.

In practice the Estate Duty Office, treating *Boden's* case as confined to goodwill, refuse to exempt on the ground of purchase a share of other assets passing to surviving partners in consideration of extra duties. There is support for this view in the Irish decision in *Re Clark* (1906), 40 Ir. L.T. 117, although it is not consistent with *A.G.* v. *Ralli, supra.*

If duty is payable under s. 2 (1) (*e*) it will be borne by the partners in whom the share vests.

An annuity payable to the widow or dependants of the deceased partner should not strictly be taken into account as part of the consideration for the purposes of s. 3, because it is not paid to the deceased, but it appears that the Estate Duty Office is prepared to do so. In fact, the provision for an annuity might make it more difficult to claim the benefit of s. 3, since it raises the question whether *full* consideration can be shown apart from the annuity. The authors believe that, where similar arrangements apply to all the partners, the mutuality of these arrangements is still full consideration in spite of the inclusion of annuities.

On the other hand, since the 1969 Act abolished s. 2 (1) (*d*) of the Finance Act, 1894, the annuity itself is not liable to any duty on the death of the partner, unless it can be charged under s. 2 (1) (*c*) on the ground that the arrangements in the partnership agreement constituted a gift of the annuity by the deceased to the dependant, and death took place within seven years after the date of the agreement. The Inland Revenue have said that they do not intend to apply s. 2 (1) (*c*) to nominations under approved pension schemes or retirement annuity contracts (see Appendix B), but the position with regard to partnership agreements is still open. A precaution that can be taken to avoid any possible claim under s. 2 (1) (*c*) is to make the annuity binding only in honour, so that the dependant has no legal claim to it. It used to be thought on the authority of *Re Miller's Agreement* [1947] Ch. 615, that an annuity payable to a dependant of a deceased partner would not give rise to estate duty, in the absence of any trust, because it was not legally enforceable. In *Beswick* v. *Beswick* [1968] A.C. 58, the House of Lords held that an annuity of this type can be enforced by the personal representatives for the benefit of the annuitant, and although the estate duty implications of this decision are obscure it is safer not to rely on *Re Miller's Agreement* as a method of creating annuities that would be outside s. 2 (1) (*c*). The desired result can be achieved by providing expressly that the annuity is to be paid in the discretion of the surviving partners, but before adopting this course the loss of tax relief to the continuing partners in certain circumstances (see p. 117) should be weighed against the possible saving of estate duty.

There are clearly estate duty advantages in providing annuities for the dependants of a deceased partner, rather than a capital sum for goodwill which will certainly be liable to estate duty.

Another question which has arisen in connection with partnership shares is whether the reduced rates of duty for agricultural property under s. 23 of the Finance Act, 1925, and for industrial hereditaments, machinery and plant under s. 28 of the

Finance Act, 1955, can be claimed in respect of partnership assets. A claim for relief on the bequest of a share of partnership plant and machinery was upheld in *Burdett-Coutts* v. *Commissioners of Inland Revenue* [1960] 1 W.L.R. 1027, and this decision has been accepted by the Revenue as being of general application to the passing of a partnership share. The result is that the reduction of 45 per cent. in the rate of duty applies to the proportion of the favoured assets included in the share.

The decision in *Burdett-Coutts* turned on the wording of the section giving relief and it does not follow that for all estate duty purposes the nature of a partnership share is the same as the underlying assets. By s. 22 of the Partnership Act, 1890, partnership land is treated as personalty in the absence of agreement to the contrary. If it is desired to preserve the character of partnership land as realty, in order that duty may be paid by instalments, it is sometimes necessary to exclude s. 22 in the conveyance to the partners or in the partnership agreement itself. Although s. 62 (2) (*c*) of the Finance Act, 1971, allows duty to be paid by instalments on an interest in land which is treated as personal property by reason of a trust for sale, it does not appear that this applies to land converted into personalty by s. 22.

However, if the land is used in the business, the privilege of paying duty by instalments will be available under another part of s. 62, on the ground that the land is an asset comprised in the net value of the business within subss. (4) and (5).

INCOME TAX

The profits of a partnership are assessed in the partnership name, but for the purpose of giving personal reliefs and charging tax the assessment is divided between the individual partners according to their shares in profits. Each partner is liable to income tax on his share, so that there is no opportunity to make any reserves at less than the full rate of tax applicable. On the other hand there is no element of double taxation as there is with company profits. The method of assessing profits of a trade or business on the preceding year basis, under Cases I and II of Schedule D, is more flexible than the corporation tax system because advantage can sometimes be taken of the commencement and discontinuance rules in ss. 115 to 118. Briefly, the assessments for the first three years are based on the profits of the first year, with an option to the taxpayer to claim assessment on actual profits of the second and third year (but not one without the other); the assessment for the final year is based on actual profits, with an option to the Revenue to assess the two preceding years (but not one without the other) on the actual profits of those years instead of on the preceding year basis. When there is a change of partners, but at least one of the previous partners stays on, s. 154 gives the taxpayers an important right to elect that the change should not be treated as a discontinuance. The election must be made within two years after the change and it must be signed by all the old and the new partners, or their personal representatives. Because of this, partnership agreements should contain a clause binding outgoing partners or their representatives to concur in the election, if so required and subject to indemnities against additional tax they incur as a result. If profits are rising steadily, it will generally pay the continuing partners to make the election and stay on the preceding year basis.

Although annual payments do not generally qualify for relief from tax at the higher rates, it is available for certain payments defined in s. 457. These include annuities to retired partners or dependants of a deceased partner, under a liability incurred for full consideration in a partnership agreement. If a new partner takes over annuity obligations in an earlier partnership agreement, his payments can also qualify for relief. In fact the tax position of continuing partners who have covenanted to pay annuities in lieu of capital sums for goodwill is satisfactory provided the annuities are for full consideration. If an annuity to a dependant binding only in honour were replaced after the partner's death by a voluntary covenant, the continuing partners would not get tax relief for the payments.

Where capital sums are paid for goodwill, they cannot be caught by s. 487, dealing with sale of income derived from personal activities, if the selling partner retires altogether. If he continues to work in the firm, the capital sums can only be caught where the selling partner is underpaid for the work he still does and the object of the exercise was tax avoidance.

CAPITAL GAINS TAX

The dealings of a partnership are treated as the dealings of the individual partners by s. 45 (7) of the Finance Act, 1965, the partners being separately assessed in respect of chargeable gains on the disposal of partnership assets. This is far more favourable than the treatment of disposals by companies, where the chargeable gain is liable to corporation tax and also serves to increase the capital gains tax on subsequent disposals by members of their shares.

The capital gains tax troubles of partners are mainly in connection with transactions between themselves. The transfer of a partnership share generally involves a disposal of a proportion of the assets of the firm, including its goodwill. The estate of a deceased partner, or a partner retiring or reducing his share, is liable to capital gains tax on any gain from the disposal, but there are a number of rules by which the gain may be minimised:

(1) Although partners are within the definition of connected persons, it is specially provided by para. 21 (4) of Sched. 7 to the Finance Act, 1965, that this is not to apply "in relation to acquisitions or disposals of partnership assets pursuant to *bona fide* commercial arrangements". This means that on a disposal between partners *inter vivos,* unless they are "connected" by family relationship as well, the chargeable gain will be measured by the actual consideration received and not by the market value of the assets. If a retiring partner transfers his share in consideration of an annuity, its value is strictly part of the consideration, but it does not appear to be Revenue practice to claim capital gains tax on a transfer of goodwill between partners except to the extent that cash is paid.

(2) When the transfer takes place on the death of a partner the exemption under Sched. 12 to the Finance Act, 1971, will be available if he was competent to dispose of his share.

(3) On the transfer of a partnership share, or part of a share, by

a partner over the age of sixty, relief can be claimed under s. 34 of the Finance Act, 1965 (pp. 46, 91).

(4) The usual arguments are available to show that goodwill, particularly of a profession or vocation, is of little or no value.

GOODWILL AND THE PROFESSIONAL PARTNERSHIP

The chief practical problem facing professional partners as a result of these various fiscal difficulties is the introduction of new blood in an age when few young men have capital to buy their shares. The authors' view is that the professions should face the realities of the situation and forget altogether the old concept of goodwill, moving instead to the conception of a continuing organism into which new partners enter without payment and from which they depart, by retirement or death, with their old age or surviving dependants looked after.

This can be achieved if the partnership agreement makes it clear that the goodwill, if any, is vested in the partners for the time being and that no-one has an asset which passes at death or is disposed of on retirement.

Thus the proportions in which profits are shared should depend upon the *ad hoc* discussions of the partners from which a retired partner would obviously be entirely dissociated. The annuities paid to retired partners should depend upon other criteria than purchase, such as length of service, earnings from the firm and so forth. To make this more practicable it may be advisable to pay definite salaries to existing partners rather than a share of profits, although of course the excess of the profits over the total salaries would still have to be shared in some agreed proportions and the "salaries" would have to be abated in some set proportions should the profits, in an evil hour, be found to be inadequate to provide the salaries. In law such salaries would still be shares and the ownership of the underlying assets of the partnership will still pass between partners and have some ascertainable value. Arranging matters so that no-one from start to finish has any goodwill which he can pass at any time removes what was usually the most valuable part of the firm's assets from the estate duty net on a partner's death or capital gains tax on retirement. His estate will still be chargeable in respect of his share of the capital assets, but this is unavoidable and more acceptable than the charge on so nebulous an asset as goodwill.

As we have seen, capital gains tax is not, as a matter of practice, charged where mutual covenants and annuities only are consideration for any change. It is arguable that no share of goodwill passes in any case because the partners earn their money and the departure of an individual merely means that someone else must earn in his place, just as employees earn their wages. There are businesses in which goodwill is a real asset, for example a restaurant with a favourable location and a known name, or a public house. It is difficult in modern times to attribute much, if any, goodwill to a professional partnership which, except in the shortest term, can only depend upon the abilities and reputation of the individual partners. If the partnership agreement contains clauses making the partnership share non-transferable and incapable of passing at death it is difficult to see how it can be taxed.

It has to be borne in mind that there is a disposal on any retirement or accession of a partner and on any re-arrangement of the partnership shares. Shares in capital assets are not necessarily altered when income shares are changed but if they are there will be a disposal for capital gains purposes. If the authors are correct, and goodwill can as a matter of valuation be eliminated, there will be no capital gains tax on any rearrangement of the shares of income of the partnership. If, however, there is in reality any sale of the right to income then inevitably this must be caught by capital gains tax and it would, on the death of a partner, be hard to argue that goodwill does not exist.

As we have seen, s. 457, which effectively kills most of the advantages of covenants in ordinary circumstances, specially excludes from its rigours annuities paid under partnership agreements, thus enabling professional partnerships to operate in a way much more analogous to a modern industrial company than has in the past been acceptable to the professions. The tax planner dealing with his own or his clients' partnership arrangements should try to set up a continuing autonomous organisation observing the following rules:

(1) Make no reference in the partnership agreement to good-

will and avoid any machinery which may quantify it as between partners.

(2) Salaries should be paid to partners and the excess in the event of profits exceeding the total salaries should, if possible, be in proportions which bear no relation to the amount of the salary paid. This is not unreasonable since everybody is at least worth in the open market a minimum salary which is most unlikely to bear any resemblance to the amount of his share under the old system of buying goodwill.

(3) No money should be paid by partners on entering the partnership except in respect of capital which will of course be returned to them on retirement.

(4) The mutual covenants as to annuities should in each case provide for two separate ones to be paid, one to the partner during his life and the other to his widow or dependants. This will ensure that the second will arise on his death and not pass on his death, thus taking advantage of the repeal of s. 2 (1) (*d*) of the Finance Act, 1894.

(5) Apart from the annuities the only cash which should pass on death or retirement should be the repayment of the share of capital subscribed by the partner.

(6) While under s. 457 an annuity can be paid to a former partner for the remainder of his life, however long, rights to payments which devolve upon others and which are payable more than ten years after he has ceased to be a partner do not benefit from the exemption in the section. Thus the widow and dependants claiming under the will or intestacy of a deceased former partner might well still be entitled under the covenant to require payment of an annuity which would not be deductible for tax at the higher rates so far as the continuing partners were concerned. The covenant should therefore provide for this eventuality.

(7) Only widows and dependants, apart from the partner himself, may be provided for under the covenants. Who are dependants is a question of fact. See *Re Baden's Deed Trusts (No. 2)* [1972] 2 All E.R. 1304.

(8) Thought should be given to the use of an unlimited company as a service company to hold the physical assets of the partnership since this might make it easier to pay out the capital

due to a retiring partner. The fact that such a company can buy its own shares could facilitate this. (See Chapter XI).

(9) It is to be remembered that the existence and possession of goodwill is a question of both law and fact. From an estate duty point of view if a partner only had the right to enjoy it during his life it would not (unless the agreement were a settlement, which seems unlikely) pass on his death. Retirement from and accessions to partnership and rearrangements of shares must, as we have seen, be disposals of goodwill if it exists. The aim of the above suggestion is to remove goodwill from the estate duty net as a matter of law and to reduce its value (if not eliminate it altogether) for capital gains tax purposes.

CHAPTER XIV

SALE OF A BUSINESS

THERE are some tax considerations which ought to be taken into account from the start of negotiations for the sale of a business, because once the substance of the transaction has been agreed it may be too late to alter the tax consequences.

If the business is being carried on by a company, the first question to decide is whether there should be a sale of shares or a sale of assets. In other words, should the purchaser buy the shares of the company from the shareholders or should he buy the goodwill and trading assets from the company?

From the point of view of the vendors it is usually better to sell shares, since this enables them to pass on to the purchaser all the ills the company is heir to; at least this is the theory, but in practice it works out differently because the purchaser will insist on the vendors giving extensive warranties about the way in which the company has been conducted and entering into indemnities against statutory apportionments of income and estate duty liability under s. 46 of the Finance Act, 1940 (p. 80). But assuming that the affairs of the company are reasonably in order, so that the warranties and indemnities can be confidently given, the advantage of selling shares is that the vendors will usually be involved in nothing worse than capital gains tax. They will not be liable to income tax on the sale unless they are assessable as dealers in shares, which is extremely unlikely, or they are caught by s. 488 of the Income and Corporation Taxes Act, 1970, which taxes certain gains of a capital nature obtained directly or indirectly from the realisation or development of land. Section 488 (11) provides a clearance procedure which it may be advisable to use when selling shares of a land-owning company. In some cases, it is also advisable to apply for clearance under s. 464, in order to make sure that the Revenue will not subsequently serve a notice under s. 460, which relates to the cancellation of tax advantages from certain transactions in securities.

Even the capital gains tax liability can sometimes be postponed by taking one of the following courses:

(1) If the purchaser is another company, it may be arranged that the vendors transfer their shares in exchange for shares issued by the purchasing company. Under para. 6 of Sched. 7 to the Finance Act, 1965, the chargeable gain on each of the orginal holdings is then rolled over into the new holding, which acquires the same base value as the original one, so that capital gains tax is payable when the new shares are sold but not before. The purchasing company does not need to be a quoted company for para. 6 to apply although the vendors will have to think carefully before accepting unquoted shares instead of cash, even if it does enable them to postpone payment of the tax. Now that death provides a new base value for capital gains tax, without being an occasion for charge, it will be possible for the tax to be avoided altogether if the shares are held until the death of a vendor.

(2) There used to be a useful provision in para. 14 of Sched. 6 to the Finance Act, 1965, dealing with payment of consideration by instalments: if the consideration taken into account in the computation was payable by instalments over a period beginning not earlier than the date of the disposal and extending for more than eighteen months, the chargeable gain was regarded as accruing in the years of assessment in which the instalments were payable and in proportion to the amounts of the instalments. This is no longer so. Section 116 of the Finance Act, 1972, amends para. 14 and provides that from 11th April, 1972, chargeable gains which under the original paragraph would have been regarded as accruing after that date will be regarded as accruing on that date. Payment of the tax which becomes chargeable on the chargeable gain then accruing may be allowed to be paid by instalments at the discretion of the Board of Inland Revenue and only in cases of "undue

hardship". It is understood that in considering whether undue hardship would arise the Revenue look primarily at the question whether the vendor could reasonably be expected to pay the tax on the full amount immediately in the light of the resources made available by the particular transaction involved. Regard will apparently not normally be paid to the other resources of the taxpayer if it can be shown that the instalment arrangement was in the circumstances, and apart from any tax consideration, a normal commercial arrangement and reflected a genuine deferment of the enjoyment of the consideration. Thus, those transactions (and they appear to have been very numerous) which have been set up since 1965 in reliance on para. 14 must now be looked at again carefully to see what adverse effects the amendment has and consideration must be given to applying to the Board for payment of the resulting tax by instalments if undue hardship can be shown. In many cases it will obviously be impossible for the taxpayer to pay the tax out of the resources made available by the transaction and it would seem that if it was not, apart from tax considerations, a normal commercial arrangement the Board will consider whether it can be found out of his other resources. This is of course not strictly tax planning since apart from the application to the Board nothing can be done to alleviate the situation, and it is mentioned here only because some reference to the tax planning possibilities of para. 14 in its old form was made in earlier editions of this book.

In the case of transactions entered into on or after 11th April, 1972, no deferment of capital gains tax is allowed by reason of the consideration being payable by instalments unless the taxpayer satisfies the Board that he would otherwise suffer undue hardship, to be interpreted in practice in the way mentioned above. The Board has no discretion here to allow payment of the tax over a period exceeding eight years.

For the purchaser a sale of shares means that he obtains a company, with its attendant problems, instead of just a business.

If the purchaser is itself a company this may not matter because the purchased company simply becomes a member of the purchaser's group. Even when an individual is buying, he may be happy to continue trading through the medium of the company, provided that his real object was not to obtain possession of the underlying assets which might be expensive in terms of tax to extract from company ownership (p. 93). In fact the advantages to the vendor of a sale of shares are usually greater than the disadvantages to the purchaser, which means that this is the method commonly adopted when the business belongs to a company, unless the company owns other assets, such as property or investments, which are not to be included in the sale of the business.

On a sale of assets, whether by a company or a partnership or a sole trader, the chief points to watch concern the apportionment of the price between the various items included in the sale.

Stock in trade: It will suit the purchaser to place as high a figure as possible on the stock, not only because articles passing by delivery do not attract stamp duty but also because the agreed sum will form the opening figure for stock in the purchaser's accounts and the higher it is the less taxable profit he will make in his first year. The vendor, while sympathising with the purchaser about stamp duty, should not forget that the agreed sum will also form the vendor's closing figure and every pound added to it means an extra pound of taxable profit. Provided the purchaser is intending to carry on the business, the agreed price is taken for the purposes of both parties' accounts and neither can afterwards claim an adjustment (s. 137 (1) (*a*)).

Plant and machinery; industrial hereditaments: Similar tax considerations apply to items qualifying for capital allowances. The purchaser will want as high a figure as possible for the starting point of his own allowances, but the higher the figure the more tax the vendor has to suffer as result of a balancing charge or a restriction of allowances. In the case of industrial buildings, the right to the allowance passes with the interest of the person who incurred the expenditure. The decision in *Woods* v. *R. M. Mallen (Engineering), Ltd.* (1969), 45 T.C. 619, shows that the wrong method of conveyancing may cause a purchaser to lose the allowance: a building erected by the vendor was sold on a sublease three days shorter than the lease held by the vendor and it was held that the purchaser had not acquired the relevant interest to support a claim for capital allowances.

Assets chargeable to capital gains tax: It will be to the advantage of the vendor to allot as much of the price as he properly can to assets held on 6th April, 1965, on which a chargeable gain can be reduced by time apportionment. This in itself will not affect the purchaser unless one of the assets is a short lease, in which case the purchaser should remember that when the duration of a lease does not exceed fifty years any expenditure on acquiring it has to be written off in accordance with the table in Sched. 8 to the Finance Act, 1965.

For a vendor of assets who is prepared to take shares in a purchasing company para. 15 of Sched. 19 to the Finance Act, 1969, mentioned on p. 90, provides a capital gains tax roll over, if the whole of the assets of the business, with the possible exception of cash, are transferred. This is similar to the roll over on the exchange of shares and results in the capital gain being wiped out if the shares are held until death. The retirement relief for a person who has reached the age of sixty under s. 34 of the Finance Act, 1965, is also available, whether the sale is of shares or assets, on the conditions described on p. 46.

Compensation for Directors and Employees

Frequently in negotiations for the sale of a family business carried on by a company the question of a "golden handshake" is mooted. Often this arises because the outgoing proprietors wish to obtain compensation for their employees or executives. Sometimes also it is felt that the directors who have been managing the business deserve some extra reward over and above the price which they will be obtaining in common with all the other shareholders. Obviously such compensation is at the expense of the general body of the shareholders because the purchaser usually has in mind a global sum and does not care whether this is paid out by way of compensation or in the price of the shares. A purchaser, however, should be warned that although the company would be the payer of compensation it will not be deductible for tax as would normally be the case with a retiring employee where it is not connected with a take-over. It was held in *Snook (James) & Co. Ltd.* v. *Blasdale* (1952), 33 T.C. 244, that the compensation was really part of the arrangements for the take-over which was obviously a capital transaction. It was made clear in that case that that circumstance alone did not of itself make such compensation non-deductible as a trading expense, but that it was essential for the company to prove that the question of such payments was considered without regard for the terms of the take-over. This would of course be difficult to prove.

In the case of an employee, if the payment is not related to his past services or to future services but is paid as consideration for the release of the employer's obligations under a service agreement, or gratuitously after the employment has ceased, it will only be taxable, if at all, under the special provision in s. 187 which requires such payments to be treated as earned income and as received on the date of termination of the employee's services. However, by s. 188 (3) the first £5,000 is exempt, increased in some cases by a further amount known as the standard capital superannuation benefit, which is calculated under complex provisions in Sched. 8. This is a most important exemption and in the majority of acquisitions of family businesses, this is the figure for compensation which appears.

CHAPTER XV

TRANSFER OF ASSETS ABROAD

1. Emigration

Anyone who wants the fullest advantage of a foreign tax system must go to live abroad and take his assets with him, so far as he is allowed to do so. If he emigrates outside the sterling area, he is subject to directions of the Bank of England, Exchange Control Department, which permit him to take only his personal chattels and £5,000 for the family unit, consisting of himself, his wife and infant children accompanying him. His remaining capital will be frozen here for four years but meanwhile he will be able to withdraw income without difficulty. The fact that he has been recognised as non-resident by the Bank of England should not lead him to think that he has achieved non-resident status for tax purposes, because this has nothing to do with exchange control. It has to be realised also that the old sterling area which embraced such famous tax-havens as Bermuda and the Bahamas has gone and most overseas countries are outside the area.

Whether he goes outside the sterling area or not, the emigrant is treated by the tax authorities as provisionally non-resident until he has satisfied them that he has given up residence in the United Kingdom. This usually takes three complete fiscal years, during which the emigrant should not make more than the briefest visits. He should also give up his home, his directorships and his other active ties with this country. Only after the inspector has agreed that non-residence has been achieved is it safe to rely on the well known practice permitting a non-resident to make visits here of less than six months in the fiscal year, so long as the average yearly visits over four years are less than three months.

Income arising in the United Kingdom, even to a non-resident, continues to be liable to income tax, except in the case of exempt Government securities or income relieved by a double tax convention.

To avoid estate duty, the emigrant must also cease to be domiciled in any part of Great Britain before he dies, and even then assets remaining here will be liable, apart from exempt Government securities or the terms of a double tax convention.

Capital gains tax liability is attracted either by residence or ordinary residence in the United Kingdom and it is immaterial, except in certain cases involving foreign domicile or double tax relief, whether the assets are situated here or abroad.

For most people, life in a tax haven is too high a price to pay for its tax advantages. For them, the question is how far tax can be saved by transferring assets abroad and continuing to live in this country. It is necessary to consider separately the position of assets held by foreign settlements, foreign companies and foreign partnerships, and finally the obstacles to be overcome before the transfer can be made at all.

2. Foreign Settlements

ESTATE DUTY

When foreign property has been settled, it is not liable to estate duty as a gift on the death of the settlor, if he was domiciled abroad either at the date of the gift or at the date of death. For this to apply the property must still be situated outside Great Britain at the date of death (*Re Kettle* [1968] 3 All E.R. 88).

The position about estate duty on the death of a beneficiary is more complicated. Under s. 28 (2) of the Finance Act, 1949, property situated outside Great Britain is not liable to estate duty if:

(1) the proper law regulating the devolution of the property or the disposition under which it passes is the law neither of England nor of Scotland, and

(2) (*a*) the beneficiary did not die domiciled in Great Britain

or

(*b*) the settlor and anyone providing funds for the settlement was domiciled outside Great Britain when the settlement took effect.

If duty on settled property is to be avoided on the death of a beneficiary, it is essential, whatever other conditions are present, to show that the proper law of the settlement is foreign. When the settled property at the date of death consists of foreign immovables, there is no problem because the proper law is always the *lex situs* (*Philipson-Stow* v. *Commissioners of Inland Revenue* [1961] A.C. 727). If foreign movables are once comprised in a settlement of which the proper law is English or Scottish, it seems that this cannot be changed unless the settlement can be terminated and the assets transferred to a new one with a different proper law.

INCOME TAX

The principal obstacle to benefiting from foreign tax systems is s. 478. The section is concerned with income which becomes payable to persons resident or domiciled abroad as a result of transfers of assets with or without associated operations. If, as a further result of the transfer with or without associated operations, an individual ordinarily resident in the United Kingdom has any power to enjoy the income of the non-resident, the individual is liable to income tax on the income of the non-resident; it is not necessary that the individual should be the person who made the transfer (*Congreve* v. *Commissioners of Inland Revenue* (1946), 30 T.C. 163).

"Power to enjoy" is very widely defined and includes any circumstances in which the income is calculated at some point of time to enure for the benefit of the individual, or in which benefits may accrue to him even though he has no rights to them at law or in equity. It seems that, even under a discretionary trust, any discretionary object ordinarily resident in the United Kingdom is liable to be assessed on income accumulated abroad by the trustees or by an underlying company, although it is difficult to imagine that the Revenue would seek to raise assessments except on people who had actually benefited or were clearly designed to be the principal beneficiaries Now that under the decision in *Macphail* v. *Doulton* (p. 37) a class of beneficiaries can be very wide there would be practical difficulties in raising assessments. It has even been facetiously suggested that the possible beneficiaries should include the Board of Inland Revenue to whom a nominal sum should be appointed to make them liable under the section. A writ of *mandamus* against the Board requiring them to raise assessments on themselves would at least add to the gaiety of life.

An individual receiving a capital sum connected with the transfer or an associated operation is dealt with by s. 478 (2), which makes him taxable on any income arising to the non-resident as a result of the transfer with or without associated operations.

The best way to reduce liability under s. 478 is to invest in property producing the minimum amount of income, or some sort of capital security such as capital shares in a "split level" trust, provided that they are not a means of receiving accumulated income, in which case there would be "power to enjoy" that income (*Latilla* v. *Commissioners of Inland Revenue* (1943), 25 T.C. 107).

CAPITAL GAINS TAX

By s. 25 (1) of the Finance Act, 1965, the trustees of a settlement are treated as a single and continuing body of persons distinct from the individuals who act as trustees from time to time. If the general administration of the trust is ordinarily carried on outside the United Kingdom and the trustees or a majority of them are not resident or not ordinarily resident in the United Kingdom the trustees as a body are not liable to capital gains tax. In other cases the body of trustees is treated as both resident and ordinarily resident and is accordingly liable to be assessed on disposal of settled property.

To these general rules there are two exceptions:

1. To help institutions and people like solicitors and accountants to compete for foreign work, there is a proviso to s. 25 (1), as amended by para. 8 (3) of Sched. 19 to the Finance Act, 1969, that a trustee carrying on a business which includes the manage-

ment of trusts is not treated as a resident of the United Kingdom if the settlor was not domiciled, resident or ordinarily resident in the United Kingdom when he made the settlement or, in the case of a settlement by will, when he died. If a majority of the trustees are treated as non-resident under the proviso, the general administration of the trusts will also be treated as carried on outside the United Kingdom, thus enabling both conditions for non-residence of the trust to be fulfilled. It should be noticed that a settlor domiciled in the United Kingdom cannot get the benefit of the proviso even if he is neither resident nor ordinarily resident when he makes the settlement; on the other hand the benefit is not lost if the settlor becomes domiciled, resident or ordinarily resident here at a later date.

2. A trust which is non-resident, whether under the general rule or the proviso, may still be caught by the anti-avoidance provisions of s. 42 of the Finance Act, 1965, if the settlor is domiciled and either resident or ordinarily resident in the United Kingdom or if he was domiciled and either resident or ordinarily resident at the date of the settlement. Note that this time domicile of the settlor by itself is not enough to cause trouble, but his status can be tested either at the date of the settlement or at the time when the chargeable gain accrues. If the section applies, the chargeable gain is assessed not on the trustees but on any beneficiary who is domiciled and either resident or ordinarily resident in the United Kingdom during the year of assessment. The gain is apportioned for this purpose between the beneficiaries according to the values of their interests. In the case of a discretionary trust a beneficiary who has received any income payments during the year in which the gain accrues, or the previous two years, is considered to have an interest equivalent to an annuity for a third of the total payments received in the three years; a discretionary object receiving a capital payment can be assessed to the extent that the payment represents an earlier chargeable gain made by the trustees.

As anti-avoidance provisions go, the section deals lightly with discretionary trusts because capital gains tax can still be deferred by withholding distributions or by timing them carefully.

One unfortunate consequence of falling within s. 42 is that a beneficiary liable to be assessed on chargeable gains of the trustees gets no corresponding relief for a capital loss.

3. Foreign Companies

ESTATE DUTY

A foreign company controlled by not more than five persons, or groups of persons, is subject to ss. 46 and 55 of the Finance Act, 1940, in the same way as a company incorporated in the United Kingdom (pp. 80–81). For example, if the deceased transferred assets situated in Great Britain to a foreign investment company, and was entitled to benefits from the company during the seven years before his death, estate duty can be assessed on the company under s. 46 and levied against the assets in Great Britain. The shareholders of a company incorporated outside the United Kingdom are also accountable, in proportion to the value of their interests in the company, for duty assessed under s. 46.

INCOME TAX

Section 478 is just as likely to catch a foreign company as a foreign trust. Perhaps the simplest application of the section is where an individual ordinarily resident in this country transfers investments to a foreign company in exchange for shares; he can then be assessed on the income of the company because his shareholding gives him "power to enjoy" its income (*Lee* v. *Commissioners of Inland Revenue* (1941), 24 T.C. 207). It will be the same if, instead of shares, he owns interest-free debentures as in *Latilla's* case (see p.132), or unsecured notes and deposits (*Lord Howard de Walden* v. *Commissioners of Inland Revenue* (1941), 25 T.C. 121). In practice, it does not seem that the Revenue apply s. 478 to a foreign trading company in which an individual ordinarily resident in the United Kingdom is interested, if the company is conducted on commercial lines.

A resident director of a foreign company is only taxed upon so much of his fees as are remitted to this country. If, therefore, they accumulate in the coffers of the company abroad, and are only remitted in a year of assessment after he has ceased to be a director or after the company has been wound up, he will not be taxed upon them.

CAPITAL GAINS TAX

In s. 41 of the Finance Act, 1965, there are anti-avoidance provisions for companies parallel to those in s. 42 applying to settlements. Chargeable gains of a non-resident company, of a sort which would be a close company if it were resident in the United Kingdom, can be apportioned among shareholders domiciled and either resident or ordinarily resident in the United Kingdom. If the part of a chargeable gain to be apportioned to a particular member is less than one-twentieth of the whole, the section does not apply to him, which suggests that a company with twenty-one equal shareholders would avoid the section altogether.

There is a noticeable emphasis in ss. 41 and 42 on domicile. The intention seems to be that only a person with a permanent connection with the United Kingdom at the relevant time should be caught by these sections.

4. Foreign Partnerships

The remarks on p.111 about the difference between partnership and joint ownership of assets apply equally to foreign partnerships, subject to any differences in the local law.

Where it is desired that investments should be held by a foreign partnership, it may be practicable for the partnership to deal in investments, in which case there can be no doubt that it is carrying on a business. The practical difficulty of such a partnership would lie in the necessity for the management and control to be situated abroad, a state of affairs not always acceptable to the resident partners. If the latter are careful only to give advice and to leave the executive action of buying and selling to the non-resident partner this should not be more than a psychological difficulty.

ESTATE DUTY

A share in a partnership is located in the country where the business is carried on, which may be relevant if the deceased was not domiciled in Great Britain or the share was included in a gift or settlement made by someone not domiciled in Great Britain (see p. 130). Otherwise there appear to be no special estate duty implications of holding assets through a foreign partnership.

INCOME TAX

Favourable treatment is given to foreign partnerships by s. 153. If the control and management of the partnership trade or business is situated abroad, the trade or business is deemed to be carried on by persons resident outside the United Kingdom, notwithstanding that some of the partners are in fact resident in the United Kingdom. This means that a person resident here, who is a partner in a firm controlled and managed abroad, will not be taxable on his share of the profits of the foreign operations except to the extent that it is remitted to the United Kingdom. If he accumulates his share of profits abroad, until he has ceased to be a partner, the accumulations can be transferred in later years of assessment without counting as a remittance. It is thought by some that to secure that a partnership is effectively controlled and managed abroad, there should be a majority of non-resident partners. The authors consider, however, that provided that all partnership decisions are taken abroad and all action is originated there, it is controlled and managed abroad. Nevertheless it is wise in such cases to have a clause in the partnership agreement requiring this procedure and there should always be at least one non-resident partner.

Section 153 expressly applies even if some of the trading operations are conducted within the United Kingdom, in which case the firm is assessable on the profits of these operations to the same extent as any other non-resident would be; a non-resident is not generally liable to United Kingdom tax on trading operations here unless a permanent establishment is maintained. Since the reference in this part of the section is to trading operations, it would not be wise for a foreign partnership carrying on a business, as distinct from a trade, to conduct any of its operations within the United Kingdom.

The position of a foreign partnership may also be favourable under s. 478, because it is thought that income paid to it would not be paid to persons resident or domiciled out of the United Kingdom. Only the non-resident partners are out of the United Kingdom and they will only be entitled to their own shares while the partners resident or domiciled here will likewise be entitled to their shares and so the main requirement of the section, that there still be power for a resident to enjoy a non-resident's income, is not satisfied. The matter is not free from doubt in view of some observations in the House of Lords in *Latilla's* case. In that case, however, all the partners were non-residents and the one under attack was a company.

CAPITAL GAINS TAX

Section 153 is applied for capital gains tax purposes by s. 45 (7) of the Finance Act, 1965. As we have seen (p. 118), partnership dealings are treated as dealings by the individual partners, so that a partner resident or ordinarily resident in the United Kingdom will be liable to capital gains tax on the disposal of a partnership asset. The effect of applying s. 153 is to make all the partners of a firm controlled and managed abroad into non-residents in relation to partnership disposals, but it does not affect ordinary residence. A partner, who for general purposes is resident but not ordinarily resident in the United Kingdom, may therefore be exempted from capital gains tax by s. 153; in the much more usual case of a partner who is ordinarily resident as well, there will be no exemption.

5. Obstacles to Transfer

The effect of the Exchange Control Act, 1947, on emigration outside the sterling area has been mentioned on p. 129. Short of emigration, or some genuine commercial reason, the Act makes it impracticable to transfer assets outside the sterling area for any of the purposes described in this chapter, and the sterling area is now a very limited one.

If the assets consist of a trade or business already carried on by a company resident in the United Kingdom, restrictions of another kind are imposed by s. 482, which makes it an offence for certain steps to be taken without the consent of the Treasury. The distinction here is between the United Kingdom and the rest of the world, without regard to the sterling area. The four cases in which Treasury consent is required under s. 482 are:

(*a*) Where a company ceases to be resident in the United Kingdom.

(*b*) Where its trade or business, or any part of it, is transferred to a non-resident. If a business is being started abroad, it is essential to make sure that this does not involve the transfer of any part of a business already carried on here by a company, unless consent is obtained. Even if this is likely to be granted, obtaining a decision is usually a protracted business.

(*c*) Where a non-resident subsidiary is caused or permitted to create or issue any shares or debentures.

(*d*) Where shares or debentures of a non-resident subsidiary are caused or permitted to be transferred to a non-resident.

The holding of investments is expressly stated to be a business for the purposes of the section, and the test of residence is the place where the central management and control of the company's trade or business is exercised.

There are severe penalties by way of imprisonment or fine for anyone who is a party to any act, even if it is only one of a series, which to his knowledge results in an offence under the section, directors of the company being presumed guilty of complicity unless they are proved innocent.

Application for consent is made by letter to the Secretary, H.M. Treasury (Department A.P.), Great George Street, London, S.W.1.

A different problem arises if the assets to be transferred are subject to an existing settlement in the United Kingdom. If the settlement gives the trustees power to release the assets to some adult member of the family, who will effect the transfer, this is the best course to adopt. If not, it may be necessary to consider whether the settlement itself can be transferred abroad.

For the purpose of avoiding capital gains tax, subject to s. 42 of the Finance Act, 1965 (p. 133), it will be sufficient that a majority of the trustees are not resident or ordinarily resident in the United Kingdom and the general administration of the trust is ordinarily carried on outside the United Kingdom. It might appear possible to achieve this result, without having to apply to the court, if a sufficient number of the trustees are willing to retire in order that a majority of non-resident trustees may be appointed, but there are three difficulties to be considered:

(*a*) A trustee who retired to facilitate an arrangement which turned out to be a breach of trust would render himself liable for that breach.

(*b*) It is not clear whether a retired trustee can be held liable under s. 8 (4) of the Finance Act, 1894, for estate duty on a subsequent death, but the Revenue claim that liability exists although they say that they will not seek to enforce it unless the duty cannot be collected from the new trustees. Until this position is clarified, a retiring trustee who hands over the assets to foreign trustees is evidently taking a risk, from which he would not be relieved even if the court approved his retirement.

(*c*) The discharge of a trustee usually depends on a new trustee being validly appointed in his place under s. 36 (1) of the Trustee Act, 1925. There is, in law, no absolute bar to the appointment of a foreign resident and at one time it was thought that if the parties were content to make the appointment out of court the retiring trustee would be discharged. Doubt has been thrown on this by the decision in *Re Whitehead's Trusts* [1971] 1 W.L.R. 833, where Pennycuick, V.-C., said "... apart from exceptional circumstances, it is not proper to make such an appointment [of persons resident abroad as trustees of an English trust] that is to say, the court would not, apart from exceptional circumstances, make such an appointment; nor would it be right for the donees of the power to make such an appointment out of court". If an appointment is not proper, in this sense, it appears to be voidable at the instance of the beneficiaries, but not invalid.

A trustee who is a member of the family may be prepared to take the risk of retiring with or without an application to the court, but a professional trustee should hesitate before doing so.

To obtain any estate duty advantage, the proper law of the trust will have to be changed. If infants or unborn persons are interested under the settlement, this can only be done by an application to the court under the Variation of Trusts Act, 1958. When the approval of the court is needed for a change of proper law, or because retiring trustees insist on an order, it is necessary to consider the exceptional circumstances in which approval will be granted. In *Re Weston's Settlements* [1969] 1 Ch. 223, the Court of Appeal refused to sanction a scheme for the appointment of new trustees in Jersey and the transfer of the funds to a new settlement to be executed there containing the same trusts as the old one. The reason for the refusal was that the connection of the family with Jersey was a recent one, and looking at the interests of the family as a whole the court did not consider that it would be for the benefit of the infants and unborn beneficiaries that the settlement should be transferred to Jersey. On the other hand, in *Re Windeatt's Will Trusts* [1969] 1 W.L.R. 692, a similar application was sanctioned by the Chancery Division where the family had established a real connection with Jersey over many years so that the fiscal advantages were not the only reason for the application.

The question in *Re Whitehead's Will Trusts* concerned the appointment of new trustees, again in Jersey, by a deed which was expressly made subject to a declaration by the court. The Vice-Chancellor said that it made no difference whether the application was under the Variation of Trusts Act, 1958, for transfer of a fund to a new settlement in a foreign country, or merely for the appointment of new trustees. Nor was there any reason why the court should not lend its assistance because "one of the purposes of this appointment is unquestionably to escape the burden of certain United Kingdom fiscal liabilities". In the result, a declaration was made that the deed duly discharged the retiring trustees, and appointed the new ones, on the ground that the principal beneficiary had lived with his family and carried on business in Jersey for the last twelve years and intended to spend the rest of his life there.

It would be wise to incorporate in any new settlement a provision giving power to some person other than the settlor to remove trustees and appoint new ones either here or abroad. This will not remove the danger under s. 8 (4) of the Finance Act, 1894, referred to above and, if there is a real possibility of the need arising, it would be as well to consider appointing a foreign trustee at thc outset.

CHAPTER XVI

THE WILL

A MAN who has taken any of the steps already discussed will find himself with less to dispose of by will than he had before, and his wife may find herself with more. Both of them should review their wills, the opportunity being taken to consider the effects of taxation on the younger generations.

All estate duty considerations in connection with wills are overshadowed by the importance of the exemption under s. 121 of the Finance Act, 1972, and the surviving spouse exemption which are dealt with in some detail in Chapter II, above. In the case of a large estate, it is essential that at least part of the estate should be disposed of so as to take advantage of these two important exemptions. There need be no practical disadvantage if property is settled so as to secure the surviving spouse exemption because the trustees of the will can be given a discretion to advance capital to the widow.

If the widow herself is a trustee, the discretion should not be exercisable at any time when she happens to be sole trustee because this would make her competent to dispose of the capital (*Re Penrose* [1933] Ch. 793). From the point of view of estate duty, this is the only danger in the power to advance capital, but it has to be carefully worded to make sure that advances will not be taxed as income in the hands of the widow. If there is any suggestion that the trustees are to make up the income of the widow to a particular figure, or enable her to maintain a particular rate of expenditure, the whole of the payments may be treated as an annuity and assessed to tax in spite of the fact that part is clearly paid out of the capital of the estate (see *Cunard's Trustees* v. *Commissioners of Inland Revenue* [1946] 1 All E.R. 159). The safest course is to give the trustees a complete discretion to make capital advances without attaching any conditions.

The surviving spouse exemption applies when the widow is given an annuity, and duty is not payable on the death of the widow if the fund out of which the annuity is payable has borne duty on the husband's death. From the tax point of view the gift of an annuity to a widow should also be approached with caution, because if the income of the estate at any time falls short of the annuity the whole amount will still be treated as the widow's income even though it has to be supplemented from capital. Although purchased annuities generally carry relief under s. 230, which exempts from tax the capital element in each instalment of the annuity, this section does not apply to annuities purchased by executors in pursuance of a direction in a will. If the benefit of the section is to be obtained, the testator must make an outright gift of a lump sum and leave it to the beneficiary to purchase an annuity if he wishes.

Discretionary Trusts and Accumulations

So far as residue is concerned, a discretionary trust in favour of children and issue, coupled with a power of accumulation, can be a benefit to the family in the same way as a discretionary trust in a settlement. Since the amendment of s. 164 of the Law of Property Act, 1925, by the Perpetuities and Accumulations Act, 1964, there is no real distinction between the periods of accumulation permissible in a will and in a settlement *inter vivos*.

It is unlikely that a testator will want to give the whole of his residue on discretionary trusts unless the children are provided for in other ways, because he will prefer his children to have fixed shares in the major part of their inheritance rather than be dependent on the exercise of a discretion, even if it is one which may save duty and tax for the family as a whole. Again, the accumulation of income may be desirable in theory, but there are few families sufficiently wealthy to abstain from the use of any substantial proportion of the income after the head of the family has died. In spite of this, consideration can always be given to the use of a discretionary trust for at least part of a large estate.

There is no income tax objection to making the surviving spouse an object of a discretionary trust created by will, since the settlor is not here to be taxed when the trust operates. Nor is there any estate duty objection, because the surviving spouse exemption prevents any charge arising under s. 2 (1) (*b*) (iii) of the Finance Act, 1894, on the death of a spouse who has received income benefits. But there is a capital gains tax anomaly which makes it undesirable for a surviving spouse to be a discretionary object as distinct from a life tenant or annuitant. Under Sched. 12 to the Finance Act, 1971, the death of a discretionary object does not give a proportionate uplift to the base value of each of the assets (p. 45) unless estate duty is actually chargeable. On the other hand, a new base value is acquired on the death of a life tenant or annuitant, even if no estate duty is chargeable because of the surviving spouse exemption.

Appropriation

The Administration of Estates Act, 1925, s. 41, gives personal representatives power to appropriate investments or other property in or towards the satisfaction of any legacy or of any other interest or share in the testator's property whether settled or not. This is a convenient power which beneficiaries often wish to see exercised, but under the section the consent of the beneficiary is normally needed. It was held in *Jopling* v. *Commissioners of Inland Revenue* [1940] 2 K.B. 282 that appropriation by consent under the section is equivalent to a purchase by the beneficiary of the appropriated property, on which *ad valorem* stamp duty has to be paid. To avoid this, the will should provide that appropriations can be made under s. 41 without any consents being given.

For capital gains tax, an appropriation of an asset to a beneficiary, in or towards satisfaction of a pecuniary legacy or an interest or share in the estate is not a disposal by the personal representatives, but the beneficiary takes the asset as legatee.

The Burden of Estate Duty

When deciding on the division of his estate a testator does not always have in mind the actual incidence of duty, but a tragic mistake may be made if large legacies are given and the residue is unintentionally swamped by duty. It will help him to make his plans if an estimate of estate duty, bearing in mind the aggregation of any gifts and settled funds, can be given to him at the start, with a reminder that unless special provision is made duty on all the chargeable gifts *inter vivos* will have to be found by the donees, duty on devises of real property will be borne by the beneficiaries, but legatees will receive their legacies duty-free at the expense of residue.

CHAPTER XVII

INSURANCE

IN tax planning insurance may be used in four ways: as a direct solution for the estate duty problem; as part of a wider scheme for reducing duty; to provide for retirement and old age; or to replace capital of a professional partnership.

Insurance as a Direct Solution for the Estate Duty Problem

As a principal remedy for estate duty, insurance is liable to be unsatisfactory, first because in the cases where it is most urgently needed it is most expensive, and secondly because policy moneys payable to the executors will themselves bear duty and so on *ad infinitum*. This does not mean that life assurance is not a useful part of long-term planning by younger people, but it is advisable that the policies should be taken out for the benefit of donees so that the estate duty advantages described in the next chapter can be obtained. These advantages are, briefly, the benefit of the seven-year rule, the sliding scale under s. 64 of the Finance Act, 1960, and the possibility of complete exemption because the premiums formed part of the normal expenditure of the deceased. In planning these policies it must be remembered that the executors will have no right to the proceeds, and that a beneficiary is not bound to make the policy moneys available for paying duty; indeed, if he is an infant, his trustees will be unable to do so unless it benefits the infant. It is advisable to see that the beneficiaries or their trustees receive the policy moneys roughly in proportion to their interests in the estate, and there will then be less difficulty in arranging for the policy moneys to be used towards payment of the duty when the time comes.

Alternatively, insurance on a man's life may be taken out by his wife, which avoids estate duty on the proceeds when he dies. If he has to give her the amounts of the premiums, these gifts may also be exempt as normal expenditure of the deceased. A wife always has an insurable interest in her husband's life, but this is not necessarily the case with other relatives. If the policy is to be held by a relative without an insurable interest, the life assured will have to take out the policy in the first place and then assign it.

Insurance as Part of a Wider Scheme for Reducing Estate Duty

A simple example of insurance as part of a wider scheme is a policy taken out by a donee to provide for the duty payable if the donor should die within seven years of the gift. The donee has an insurable interest for this purpose, since the duty is payable by him, and the rate may be high as a result of aggregation of the gift with other property passing on the death. Quotations can be obtained for policies reducing after four, five and six years in accordance with s. 64 of the Finance Act, 1960.

These decreasing term policies are often taken out in connection with variations of trusts. On the increase of the five-year period to seven in 1968, the Government gave an undertaking that trustees who had distributed funds in reliance on a five-year insurance would not be held responsible for duty if death occurred within the extended period; the Estate Duty Office will look only to the beneficiaries.

A more complicated case is the use of whole life assurance in combination with an immediate annuity. The first step is for the proposer to realise his assets and use the proceeds to buy a substantial annuity on his own life. The capital element in a purchased annuity is exempt from tax under s. 230; the capital element means the proportion of the annuity payments which represents return of the purchase price, as distinct from interest on it, and for the purposes of a rough estimate this proportion can be taken as a percentage equal to the annuitant's age at the date of purchase. For example, if a man of sixty-five buys an annuity, the capital element will be about 65 per cent. and only 35 per cent. of each annuity payment will be taxable.

The second step is to compensate the dependants for their expectations in the capital which has been laid out on the purchase of the annuity. This is done by the proposer taking policies on his own life in favour of the dependants, bearing in mind that the proportion of the proceeds dutiable will begin to diminish as soon as he has survived the transaction by more than four years, by the joint effect of s. 34 of the Finance Act, 1959, and s. 64 of the Finance Act, 1960, described in the next chapter. The insurance may be expensive, but the annuity provides surplus income for the payment of the premiums and as an additional incentive the normal income tax relief on the premiums can be claimed.

The former advantages of this scheme have been much reduced by the abolition of non-aggregation of property in which the deceased never had an interest, except for the first £25,000 of insurances made before 20th March, 1968 (s. 38 of the Finance Act, 1968). What is more, s. 37 (2) of the Finance Act, 1968, directly attacks the combined scheme by denying any exemption from estate duty on the ground that the premiums, or gifts to pay the premiums, were normal expenditure of the deceased, unless it can be shown that the insurance and the purchase of the annuity were not associated operations.

In practice the Estate Duty Office apply s. 37 (2) leniently and do not regard the annuity and the policy as associated operations if the policy was issued after full evidence of health had been obtained and on terms which would have been the same if the annuity had not been bought.

One way to operate the combined scheme is for the wife to take out the insurance on her husband's life, provided she can pay the premiums out of her own income.

Insurance to Provide for Retirement and Old Age

Anyone who has yielded to the advice of tax planners is likely to find that he has put the bulk of his savings beyond his own reach, and he will be anxious to know how far he can provide by insurance for his own retirement and old age, without paying the premiums out of fully taxed income. There are three ways in which this may be achieved:

(*a*) If the client is a director or executive of a company, the most advantageous method is a retirement benefits scheme approved by the Inland Revenue under ss. 19 and 20 of the Finance Act, 1970. This may be a scheme covering several directors or employees, or a separate agreement for one person; it is generally non-contributory and once approval has been given for a scheme established under irrevocable trusts the cost of the provision is allowed against the company's tax. The main benefit must be in the form of pensions, but a lump sum up to one and a half times the final salary can be taken on retirement.

The value of the benefits is limited to one-sixtieth of the retiring salary, multiplied by the number of years' service up to a maximum of forty. As mentioned on p. 77, service as a controlling director need no longer be excluded, in the case of retirement benefit schemes which come into force or are altered after 5th April 1973. The Inland Revenue have issued practice notes dated 6th June 1973, under which some restriction is still placed on a director who holds more than 20% of the voting rights in the company; shares held by his wife, his infant children or his family trustees count towards the 20%. In these cases the pension cannot be based solely on the final year's remuneration, the suspicion being that the director might be able to arrange for his salary in his last year to be increased purely for pension reasons.

This type of provision is also favourable for estate duty, because benefits paid to dependants will not be liable to duty unless the deceased was competent to dispose of them. The Inland Revenue has issued helpful notes on the liability to estate duty of benefits under superannuation schemes, which are reproduced in Appendix B.

(*b*) Section 226 as extended by s. 20 of the Finance Act, 1971, enables controlling directors (except of investment companies), partners and anyone with earnings from non-pensionable employment to provide for retirement annuities under contracts approved by the Inland Revenue. Premiums paid under approved contracts are allowed against income tax and surtax to the extent of 15 per cent. of the net relevant earnings, or a maximum of £1,500 per annum, with slight extensions for those born before 1916. To the extent that a premium fails to qualify because it exceeds the permitted percentage, the excess may be carried forward to future years until it is absorbed, but no carry forward is allowed of the excess of a premium over the maximum figure.

The benefit must generally take the form of:

(i) a life annuity for the taxpayer commencing between the ages of sixty and seventy, with or without secondary annuities for a widow or dependants and return of contributions on death if no annuity becomes payable, or

(ii) a similar annuity for the wife or husband or one or more dependants, or

(iii) a lump sum payable to the taxpayer's personal representatives on his death before the age of seventy.

In the case of contracts approved under (ii) or (iii) the total premiums allowable in one year cannot exceed 5 per cent of the net relevant earnings or a maximum of £500; these premiums also count towards the overall limits of 15 per cent. and £1,500.

An approved contract is allowed to contain commutation rights, under which the taxpayer can elect, at or before the time when the annuity first becomes payable to him, to take a lump sum not exceeding three times the annual amount of the remaining annuity.

The advantage of retirement annuities lies in the extreme flexibility of the contracts offered by insurance companies, which enables the contributor to vary his premium each year according to his earnings, or to miss it altogether; each premium which he does pay secures a corresponding annuity commencing at the agreed age. Most contracts provide for return of contributions on death before the pension age, which can usefully be combined with a diminishing life cover. Diminishing life policies are comparatively cheap, and the cover can be arranged so that, on death before pension age, the combined life insurance and return of annuity premiums will produce a constant sum, provided regular premiums are paid. There are also schemes which link retirement annuities to unit trusts in order to provide some protection against inflation.

(*c*) Quite apart from the terms of his employment or the amount of his earnings, any individual is entitled to relief against income tax, at the basic rate only, for life assurance premiums paid by him or his wife within certain limits set out in ss. 19 and 21 as amended by s. 33 (3) of the Finance Act, 1971, and provided, in the case of assurances made after 19th March, 1968, that the policy is a qualifying policy within Part 1 of Sched. 1. The allowance is limited to the *smallest* of:

One half of the premiums (a higher proportion is allowed if the total premiums are less than £20); or

One sixth of the taxpayer's total income; or

Seven per cent. of the sum assured by each policy.

The assurance must have been made originally by the taxpayer on the life of himself or his wife, but it does not matter that the policy no longer belongs to him at the date of payment of the premium, for instance, if it has been assigned to trustees or to a partner. Provided that a capital sum is assured on death the premiums carry relief to the extent mentioned, even though the life cover is combined with endowment assurance and the premiums relate to both. In this way income tax relief can be obtained on premiums paid under a policy securing a lump sum on retirement, which can be used to purchase an annuity when the time comes. In some cases this is a cheaper way of providing an annuity on retirement than a contract approved under s. 226, with the added advantage of being able to keep the lump sum if this is preferred to an annuity.

The restrictions relating to qualifying policies are aimed at single-premium and other artificial types of life policy. To qualify for the basic rate income tax relief, premiums must comply with the conditions in Pt. I of Sched. 1, which means roughly that they must be payable at yearly or shorter intervals over a period which will last for at least ten years, unless death or disability occurs earlier, the premiums being spread so that the amount payable in any twelve months is not more than twice the amount payable in any other twelve months or more than one-eighth of the total payable over the ten years. There is a special provision for term policies of less than ten years, which must not have a surrender value of more than the premiums paid.

While these restrictions hold no terrors for genuine life and endowment assurance, the penalties for ignoring them are drastic. Not only is basic rate income tax relief on the premiums withdrawn, but by s. 393 tax at the higher rates is charged on any gain arising in connection with a policy that does not qualify. A gain in this context means the amount obtained when the policy matures, or when it is surrendered or assigned, less the total of premiums that have been paid. If the policy matures on death, the gain is only the surrender value immediately before death less premiums, thus preserving from higher rate tax the benefit of the true risk element.

The higher rate tax is charged on the beneficial owner of the policy, but if the policy is held by trustees the tax falls on the settlor, however long ago the settlement was made.

Insurance to Replace Capital of a Professional Partnership

When a partner dies or retires, his share of capital must eventually be withdrawn from the firm. To replace this money, and possibly to pay capital sums for the outgoing partner's share of goodwill at the same time, is a particularly difficult problem for a professional firm with no assets on which it can readily borrow.

The solution may be for each partner to take out an endowment policy on his own life in trust for his partners, the endowment being geared to the age of retirement. If the policies are taken in trust from the beginning, there is no need for cross-assignments which might give rise to capital gains tax on the ground that the policies had been transferred for value. A partner paying the premiums on the policy he has taken out can claim income tax relief, but when the policy matures the proceeds will be in the hands of the continuing partners to enable them to meet their obligations.

If each partner has agreed to pay an equal premium, the policy maturing on death should be exempt from duty under the purchase exemption, although there will be some duty to pay on the surrender values of the other policies to the extent that they are held in trust for the deceased.

The payment of equal premiums may not produce sufficient on the death or retirement of the older partners, in which case the younger partners can supplement the cover by taking out life-of-another policies on their seniors. Life-of-another policies do not carry any income tax reliefs for premiums, but on the other hand the proceeds are not liable to estate duty.

An alternative plan, which is easier to apply but provides no income tax relief, involves each partner taking out:

(*a*) an endowment assurance on the life of each partner who is older than himself, to mature on the expected retirement age of that partner and thus provide funds for paying him out, and

(*b*) a temporary life cover on each partner who is younger than himself, to provide funds in the event of that partner dying before the expected retirement age of the proposer.

The replacement of working capital, and the provision of capital sums for purchase of goodwill, should not be confused with the separate question of pensions for outgoing partners or their dependants as a *substitute* for capital payments for goodwill. Pensions can be provided either by retirement annuities or by endowment assurance, but this means each partner bearing the cost of his own provision. For most firms it is no solution to the goodwill problem, unless the partnership shares are revised so that the senior partners are given additional income out of which to pay their premiums. A logical scheme on these lines can be worked out, but it may not be possible to apply it to all the partners of a firm with a wide spread of ages, because this would leave the junior partners with too low a share to be practicable.

The chief practical disadvantage of life assurance policies for partnership purposes is that to be effective they should be taken out when the partners are young, but this is precisely the time when their domestic burdens are likely to be heaviest and their income from the firm smallest. In these inflationary times there is the further disadvantage that the benefits which eventually become payable have so diminished in real value that they bear little relationship to the burden which the premiums represented in earlier years.

The treatment of life assurance policies for estate duty is more fully dealt with in the next chapter.

CHAPTER XVIII

LIFE POLICIES AND ESTATE DUTY

A LIFE policy may become liable to estate duty on the death of the life assured in any one of four ways:

(1) *Because it forms part of his estate*

If the policy belonged to the deceased at the date of death, then it is dutiable, under s. 2 (1) (*a*) of the Finance Act, 1894, like any other property of which he was competent to dispose. The value of the policy for estate duty is the total of the policy moneys and any bonuses.

(2) *As settled property*

If the policy was comprised in a settlement and the deceased had a beneficial interest in possession during the seven years ending with his death, there will be a claim under s. 2 (1) (*b*).

(3) *As a gift* inter vivos *of the policy*

A policy which belonged to the deceased and was given away by him within seven years of his death, or in which he reserved a benefit, will be liable to duty under s. 2 (1) (*c*) in the same circumstances as any other gift. The donee will have the benefit of s. 64 of the Finance Act, 1960, by which the value of the property is reduced for purposes of duty on a sliding scale once the donor has survived an effective gift by more than four years. The policy will be valued for duty by reference to the premiums paid before the date of the gift, as explained later, under s. 34 (3) of the Finance Act, 1959.

(4) *As a gift of rights under the policy*

This head of charge depends on the combined effect of s. 2 (1) (*c*) of the 1894 Act and s. 34 of the Finance Act, 1959. It is the only one applying exclusively to life policies.

Section 34 applies when the deceased has paid by way of gift a premium on a policy on his own life and the payment operates to keep up the policy for the benefit of another person. The policy may be one which the deceased gave to the donee or one which was originally taken out in the donee's name. In such cases each payment is treated as a gift of "rights under the policy" and these rights are valued at the date of death by applying the following formula:

> Take the total of all *relevant premiums*.
>
> Find the proportion which the payment in question bears to that total.
>
> Apply that proportion to the *value of the policy*.
>
> The answer is the value of the rights under the policy attributable to the payment.

In the straightforward case where the policy is held by the donee until maturity, the *relevant premiums* are all the premiums paid on the policy and the *value of the policy* is the total of the benefits receivable on maturity. In the more complicated case where the donee has dealt with the policy or surrendered it after the payment of the premium in question, the *relevant premiums* are those paid before the dealing or surrender and the *value of the policy* has to be ascertained at the time of the dealing or surrender. This is in keeping with the general rule for the valuation of gifts. The effect so far is that each payment of a premium within the seven-year period causes a corresponding slice of the policy to become liable to duty. Possibly the payment of a premium outside the seven-year period would have the same result if the deceased were not excluded from any benefit in the rights under the policy, but how this would apply is far from clear.

The section then goes on to deal in subs. (3) with cases where there has been a gift of the policy itself. It is not necessary to use the conception of "rights under the policy" here, because a gift of a policy is dutiable under the same circumstances as any other gift *inter vivos* as we have already noticed, but what the subsection does is to introduce a rule for *valuation* of policies given away. Where a policy is chargeable as having been the subject of a gift within the seven-year period, or because a benefit was reserved, the property deemed to pass is to be valued by reference to the *value of the policy,* in the proportion borne by the total premiums paid before the gift to the total of all *relevant premiums*.

The interaction of these two provisions is probably worth an illustration:

1st July, 1972	*A* takes out policy on own life for £1,000 and pays first premium of £50.
1st July, 1973	*A* pays premium of £50.
1st July, 1974	*A* pays premium of £50.
1st July, 1975	*A* pays premium of £50.
1st Jan., 1976	*A* gives policy to *B*.
1st July, 1976	*A* pays premium of £50 by way of gift.
1st July, 1977	*A* pays premium of £50 by way of gift.
1st July, 1978	*B* pays premium of £50 himself.
1st July, 1979	*B* pays premium of £50 himself, the policy becoming fully paid.
5th April, 1982	*A* dies and the policy matures.

The gift of the policy itself in 1976 attracts duty under s. 2 (1) (*c*) and the property deemed to pass is valued at one-half the total proceeds of the policy, because at the date of the gift *A* had paid £200 in premiums, which turned out to be one-half of the total premiums. The payments of premium by *A* in 1976 and 1977 also attract duty as gifts of rights under the policy, each of these gifts being valued at one-eighth of the total proceeds of the policy because eight premiums were paid in all.

Section 64 of the Finance Act, 1960, now comes into play. The graduated relief applies to the gift of the policy in 1976, and to avoid doubt it is also expressly extended to a payment of a premium which is treated as a gift under s. 34 of the 1959 Act. The gift of the policy has been survived by six years, which means that the value is reduced for estate duty by 60 per cent. The payments of premiums have been survived by five and four years and their value is reduced by 30 and 15 per cent. As a final result duty is charged on:

$$\left(\frac{£1{,}000}{2} \times \frac{40}{100}\right) + \left(\frac{£1{,}000}{8} \times \frac{70}{100}\right) + \left(\frac{£1{,}000}{8} \times \frac{85}{100}\right)$$

$$= £393 \cdot 75$$

Even this charge could be avoided if it were shown that the premiums were part of the normal expenditure of the deceased (see p.11).

The exemption contained in s. 33 of the Finance Act, 1949, for gifts not exceeding £500 in the case of any one donee can apply to duty which would otherwise be charged on a policy, or rights under a policy, but these have to be valued at the date of each gift in order to see whether the total exceeds £500.

Section 34 refers to the payment of a premium which operates to "keep up" the policy for the benefit of another person. A single premium policy is not kept up by the payment of the single premium since the policy is fully paid from the start; "keeping up" suggests a series of payments to prevent a policy already in existence from lapsing. If this argument is correct, s. 34 does not apply to the payment of a single premium to effect a policy for the benefit of another person, but the transaction can probably be treated on ordinary principles as a gift of the policy, liable to duty in the event of death with seven years (*Ralli Bros. Trustee Co., Ltd.* v. *Commissioners of Inland Revenue* [1968] Ch. 215).

Non-aggregation

Before the Finance Act, 1968, the great advantage of policies liable to duty under s. 34 of the Finance Act, 1959, was the possibility of obtaining non-aggregation by writing the policy under the Married Women's Property Act, 1882, or on similar trusts. Non-aggregation, on the ground that the deceased never had an interest in the property, has been abolished, the only exception being for the first £25,000 of policies effected before 20th March, 1968.

The result is that someone paying a premium by way of gift to keep up a policy on his life for the benefit of a donee can no longer secure for his estate the benefit of non-aggregation, whether he ever had an interest in the policy or not, apart from the excepted case. On the other hand, these policies are still a useful way of providing for dependants, because the effect of premiums paid begins to fall out of account after four years and above all because there is the possibility that premiums will be treated as normal expenditure of the deceased.

The circumstances to which the four heads of charge apply, and the principal results of their application, are summarised in Appendix A.

Capital Gains Tax

No chargeable gain arises on the disposal of a life policy, or when it falls in, unless it has by that time come into the hands of a purchaser for money or money's worth (s. 28 of the Finance Act, 1965).

APPENDIX A

LIFE POLICIES: HEADS OF CHARGE TO ESTATE DUTY, ETC.

Circumstances	*Head of Charge*	*Property charged*	*Whether charge graduated under the Finance Act, 1960, s. 64*	*Whether property aggregable*
Policy belonging to estate	Finance Act, 1894, s. 2 (1) (*a*)	Full value of policy	Not applicable	Yes
Settled policy	s. 2 (1) (*b*)	Proportion of value according to extent of beneficial interest during 7 years before death (Finance Act, 1969, s. 37)	Yes	Yes
Gift of policy within seven years of death (or donor not excluded)	s. 2 (1) (*c*)	Proportion of value of policy according to premiums paid at date of gift (Finance Act, 1959, s. 34 (3))	Yes	Yes
Payment by way of gift of premium within seven years of death	s. 2 (1) (*c*) and Finance Act, 1959, s. 34	Rights under the policy	Yes	Yes, subject to limited exception for pre-20th March, 1968, policies, in which deceased never had an interest

APPENDIX B

ESTATE DUTY ON BENEFITS UNDER EMPLOYEES' SUPERANNUATION SCHEMES

The notes set out in this Appendix have been prepared by the Inland Revenue in order to explain in general terms the practice of the Estate Duty Office regarding liability to estate duty on lump sums and annuities payable on death under the rules of employees' retirement benefits schemes and superannuation funds and under retirement annuity contracts and trust schemes approved under s. 22 of the Finance Act, 1956 [now s. 226].

Payments to Deceased's Legal Personal Representatives

1. Payments that are legally due to the legal personal representatives and cannot be withheld from them at the discretion of any person exercisable after the death are liable to duty as part of the deceased's free estate. The legal personal representatives are accountable for the duty under s. 8 (3) of the Finance Act, 1894.

2. Amounts liable to duty under this head are subject to normal aggregation with other property passing on the death for the purpose of determining the rate of duty.

Where Deceased had General Power of Nomination

3. Where the deceased had a general power to nominate a benefit to anyone he wished and he had not exercised his power irrevocably in his lifetime, the benefit is liable to duty under s. 2 (1) (*a*) of the Finance Act, 1894, and the legal personal representatives are accountable for the duty under s. 8 (3).

4. The case where the deceased had at the time of his death an option to have a sum of money paid to his legal personal representatives normally falls under this head. Where, however, an annuity is payable to the deceased's widow, widower or dependant under a contract or trust scheme approved under s. 22 of the Finance Act, 1956, and the deceased had an option to have a sum of money paid instead to his legal personal representatives, duty is not charged under this head (s. 39 (2) of the Finance Act, 1957).

5. Amounts liable to duty under this head are subject to normal aggregation with other property passing on the death.

* * * * *

16. A benefit which escapes duty under one of the above heads may, of course, be liable to duty under another head.

The following supplemental notes outline the effects of the estate duty changes made by the Finance Act, 1969 (which apply to deaths on or after 16th April, 1969) and also deal with two other aspects of liability.

A. Payments to the Deceased's Legal Personal Representatives

B. Where the Deceased had a General Power of Nomination

The Finance Act, 1969, has no effect on the liability to estate duty:

(*a*) of payments legally due to the legal personal representatives which cannot be witheld from them at the discretion of any person exercisable after the death; or

(*b*) where the deceased had a general power to nominate a benefit to anyone he wished and had not exercised his power irrevocably in his lifetime.

Paragraphs 1 to 5 of the original notes therefore remain valid. As stated, the personal representatives are accountable where benefits are liable to duty under these heads and should include the benefits in the Inland Revenue Affidavit of the deceased's estate.

Where a payment falling within paragraph (*a*) is made to the duly constituted legal personal representatives, the person making the payment need not send a separate notification to the Estate Duty Office.

C. Annuities which Continue to be Payable after the Deceased's Death

The effect of s. 36 (1) of the 1969 Act is that s. 1 of the Finance Act, 1894, no longer operates as an independent charging section. Liability to estate duty arises only where property falls within one of the paragraphs of s. 2 (1) of the 1894 Act, or within other statutory provisions imposing a charge of duty.

Accordingly duty will no longer be chargeable on an annuity subsisting as a separate item of property and continuing after the death, as property "passing" on death under s. 1, and paras. 6 to 8 of the original notes are withdrawn.

If after the death the annuity is payable to the deceased's legal personal representatives, it will, of course, be chargeable under paragraph A.

D. Interests Provided by the Deceased

Section 2 (1) (*d*) of the Finance Act, 1894, the former charge on annuities or other interests purchased or provided by the deceased to the extent of the beneficial interest accruing or arising on his death, is repealed by the Finance Act, 1969. No charge of estate duty now arises in the circumstances described in paras. 9 to 15 of the original notes, and these paragraphs are also withdrawn.

E. Death of Pensioner or Annuitant

It has never been the official practice to claim duty under s. 2 (1) (*b*) of the Finance Act, 1894, on the cesser of a pension or annuity payable under approved superannuation arrangements, even where the benefit was charged on the assets of a fund. Paragraph 10 (*c*) of Pt. II of Sched. 17 to the Finance Act, 1969, now expressly exempts pensions and annuities of this kind from any liability under the substituted s. 2 (1) (*b*) of the 1894 Act (which imposes the new charge of estate duty on settled property). The sub-paragraph provides that the new charge is not to apply by reason of an interest of the deceased under such a scheme or in such a fund as is described in s. 387 (1) or (2) of the Income Tax Act, 1952, being an interest by way of pension or annuity. The exemption covers not only statutory superannuation schemes and schemes and funds approved by the Inland Revenue but also certain schemes and funds which, because of the date when they were set up or of the level of remuneration of the employees concerned, did not require formal approval.

The concluding part of para. 10 (*c*) makes it clear that the exemption does not extend to the death of a person who had an interest under a trust (or who benefited under a discretionary trust) of a *lump sum* benefit payable under a scheme or fund. If a lump sum benefit is settled (for example, in the exercise of discretionary powers as to the disposal of a death benefit), a claim for duty may arise on the death of any beneficiary under the settlement.

F. Payments Made in Exercise of a Discretion

Where a lump sum benefit payable under a scheme or fund is not settled but is distributed in exercise of a discretion exercisable after the death, the death of a person to whom a payment is made will not give rise to any liability under the substituted s. 2 (1) (*b*).

G. Gifts Inter Vivos

It is not the official practice to claim estate duty under s. 2 (1) (*c*) of the Finance Act, 1894, as a gift *inter vivos*, on any benefit payable under superannuation arrangements such as are referred to in para. 10 (*c*) of Pt. II of Sched. 17 to the 1969 Act (see E. above) or under an approved retirement annuity contract or trust scheme. This is so even if the benefit arises as a result of the surrender by the deceased, within seven years of his death, of part of a benefit to which he would have been entitled, as where an employee gives up part of his retirement pension in exchange for an annuity for his widow to begin on his death.

This practice does not extend to any *separate* provision made by an employee for his dependants or others, for example under a group life insurance scheme operated in conjunction with superannuation arrangements. Premiums paid by the deceased on a policy on his life effected under a scheme of this kind may be chargeable to duty as gifts *inter vivos,* although the gifts will commonly qualify for exemption under s. 37 of the Finance Act, 1968, as normal income gifts.

The following note has been prepared and issued on behalf of the Board (September 1972):

Estate Duty

1. This note has been prepared at the request of The National

Association of Pension Funds primarily to enable the administrators of pension schemes to answer enquiries about the Estate Duty liability of benefits payable on death under such schemes.

2. No liability to Estate Duty arises in respect of benefits payable on a person's death under his pension scheme except in the circumstances explained below.

3. Such benefits are liable to Estate Duty if:

(*a*) they form part of his freely disposable property passing under his will or intestacy. (This applies only if his executors or administrators have a legally enforceable claim to the benefits: if they were payable to them only at the discretion of the trustees of the pension fund or some similar persons they are not liable to estate duty)

or

(*b*) he had the power, immediately before his death, to nominate or appoint the benefits to anyone he pleased.

In these cases the benefits should be included in the Inland Revenue Affidavit (schedule of the deceased's assets) which has to be completed when applying for a grant of probate or letters of administration. The Estate Duty (if any) which is assessed on the Inland Revenue Affidavit has to be paid before the grant can be obtained.

4. Such benefits may also be liable to Estate Duty if the pension scheme is contributory although, in practice, benefits payable under a contributory scheme which has been approved for income tax purposes are not considered to be so liable. Benefits payable under a contributory scheme which has not been so approved, or under a scheme which does not make any provision for a member's retirement should be mentioned in reply to the question in the Inland Revenue Affidavit about gifts inter vivos. Estate Duty need not be paid on the benefits before obtaining the grant of probate or letters of administration. If Estate Duty proves to be payable on the benefits the Estate Duty Office will communicate with the persons liable to pay the duty.

APPENDIX C

ESTATE DUTY—
DISCRETIONARY TRUSTS

1. The Board of Inland Revenue have had representations that trustees and their professional advisers are uncertain about the kind of records that trustees will need to maintain in the light of the legislation imposing a charge on discretionary trusts (ss. 36 and 37 of the Finance Act, 1969, as amended by s. 31 of the Finance Act, 1970). This statement indicates the practice of the Estate Duty Office in relation to some aspects of the legislation which affect the matter.

2. Broadly, estate duty is payable on the death of a beneficiary under a discretionary trust on the same proportion of the trust property as the proportion that the deceased received of the trust income arising during a specified period of up to 7 years (the relevant period as defined in s. 37, running to the date of death, or the date of advance out of the settled funds, etc).

3. In the context, "income" is considered to be income determined on ordinary trust principles. It is not, e.g., income as ascertained for income tax purposes. The Revenue view is that it is income net of income tax which the trustees are liable to pay, and net of any income which trustees must properly retain as a provision against future or contingent liabilities falling upon income, such as surtax which is levied on the settlor and which he can reclaim from the trustees.

Under s. 36 (6) (*d*) of the Finance Act, 1969, costs, expenses and fees properly payable out of income are to be deducted from the income. They are considered to be payable at the time when they become due and payable even if they are not in fact paid until later.

4. The term "arising" (during the relevant period) is considered, in the case of income consisting of dividends, interests, rent etc., to mean "received by the trustees". This means that neither dividends nor other income received in respect of a period spanning the beginning or end of a relevant period need be apportioned. In some cases, e.g., an unincorporated business or a landed estate, it will be sufficient to use the normal periodical accounts of the business or estate; income for broken periods at the beginning and end of the relevant period may be estimated by a time apportionment or such other method as seems reasonable in the particular circumstances.

5. Section 37 (3) (*b*) of the Finance Act, 1969, provides the test for deciding once and for all whether, and to what extent, a payment made to a discretionary beneficiary is a payment of income or capital. If it is an income payment it may become part of the numerator of the fraction which determines how much of the trust fund is dutiable on his death. If

it is a capital payment and was made after 15th April, 1969, parts of it may become liable to estate duty on the deaths within the next 7 years of any of the other discretionary beneficiaries, and the trustees, who will be accountable for any such estate duty, may wish to obtain from the Estate Duty Office a certificate under s. 44 (3) of the Finance Act, 1950, which quantifies their liability.

The test requires regard to be had to all income subject to the discretionary trust arising since 15th April, 1963, up to the time of the particular payment in question and provides that the payment is to be treated as income to the extent that there was a balance of income at that time sufficient to cover it after allowing for all previous payments since 15th April, 1963, treated as income payments. For the purpose of the test, all income available during the period for distribution under the discretion is included whether it derives from the original trust fund or from accumulations or accretions subsequently added to it; there is no need to separate the income according to its sources.

Trustees need therefore to analyse their past accounts on this basis and keep a note of any income payments made to discretionary beneficiaries during the period 15th April, 1963, to 15th April, 1969, and of any unexhausted balance of income available for future distribution at the end of that period.

Beginning with 16th April, 1969, a similar analysis should in strictness be made whenever a payment is made. In practice it may be sufficient to make a formal analysis only when there is any uncertainty as to the status of a payment under the test. The figures required by such an analysis are:

(1) any unexhausted balance of income brought forward from the last analysis;

(2) the income received during the intervening period, and

(3) all payments made during that period.

APPENDIX D

APPORTIONMENT OF INCOME OF CLOSE COMPANIES

1. The following notice issued by the Board in February, 1973, sets out the Revenue Practice with regard to the Statutory Apportionment of the Income of Close Companies:

STATEMENT OF PRACTICE

CLOSE COMPANIES

The purpose of this statement is to bring together various statements of practice relating to the taxation of close companies and to re-state them in the light of the introduction of the new system of corporation tax on 6th April, 1973. References to the earlier statements are shown in parenthesis.

1. Liability to Apportionment of Income of Groups of Companies

In arriving at the relevant income of a parent company which is a trading company (or a "member of a trading group" as defined by paragraph 11 (2) of Schedule 16, Finance Act, 1972) regard will be had so far as is reasonable to the business requirements and resources of companies which are subsidiaries of the parent company and are trading companies or members of the trading group. This approach may need to be modified in particular cases, for example, where persons other than the parent company have a substantial interest in some or all of the subsidiary companies.

In arriving at the relevant income of a subsidiary company which is a trading company or a member of the trading group, the subsidiary company's requirements would normally be limited to those of its own business, but regard will be had to the requirements and resources of other companies in the group if it is appropriate to do so, for example, where the subsidiary company has trading links with the parent company or with another subsidiary in the group. (Press Statement, 13th July, 1970.)

2. Associated Companies

In determining whether two companies are controlled by the same persons, and are therefore associated for the purposes of applying the provisions of paragraph 9 of Schedule 16, Finance Act, 1972 (abatement of estate or trading income in determining maximum relevant income) it is not normally the practice to seek to attribute to a person the rights and powers of his relatives (other than his wife and minor children). If, for example, one individual owned all the shares in company A, and his brother owned all the shares in company B, it will not normally be contended that B's powers could be attributed to A so that A could be treated as controlling B's company as well as his own. Again, if their father held, say, 20 per cent. of the shares in each son's company, it will not normally be contended that the powers of the sons should be attributed to him so that he could be regarded as controlling both companies. It will be necessary, however, to reserve for consideration all cases where there was a substantial trading interdependence between the two companies. Cases where companies would be associated if a person had attributed to him the rights and powers of persons who were his associates under Section 303 (3) (*b*) and (*c*), Income and Corporation Taxes Act, 1970, will be considered on their facts. There may be some exceptional cases where, without attributing to any person the rights and powers of his associates, two or more companies could be regarded as associated because both are controlled by the same trustee (for example, the trustee company of a clearing bank). This fact alone will not be regarded as a ground for treating such companies as associated; but if there were any connection, past or present, between the companies, the case would need to be considered on its facts. Similarly it will not be contended that two or more companies are associated merely because they could all be treated (under Section 302 (2) to (4), Income and Corporation Taxes Act, 1970, as amended by paragraph 5 of Schedule 17, Finance Act, 1972) as controlled by the same loan creditor, provided that the loan creditor is an open company (or any other bona fide commercial loan creditor, and there is no other connection between the companies). (Board's letter 25th July, 1968, to the Accountants' Joint Parliamentary Committee.)

N.B.—This practice will also be applied for determining whether two companies are controlled by the same persons, and thus associated, for the purposes of Section 95, Finance Act, 1972 (mitigation of corporation tax liability of small companies).

3. TREATMENT OF DIVIDENDS PAID WITHIN A GROUP IN DETERMINING DISTRIBUTABLE PROFITS FOR THE PURPOSES OF APPORTIONMENT OF COMPANY INCOME

Where a group of close companies so wishes, all distributions within the group, for all periods, shall be included in the distributable profits of the periods for which they are payable (apart from distributions made more than a reasonable time after the end of the period, i.e. those falling outside paragraph 10 (1) (*a*) of Schedule 16, Finance Act, 1972). For this purpose a group of companies will be regarded as consisting of a parent company which is not itself a subsidiary of another company, and all companies (including companies not resident in the United Kingdom) which are subsidiaries of that parent ("subsidiary" being interpreted in accordance with Section 284 (5), Income and Corporation Taxes Act, 1970, but disregarding subparagraph (5) (*c*)).

Where a group of close companies wishes to adopt this basis it will be required to give an undertaking that the basis will be adhered to irrevocably as long as companies remain within the group. To avoid transitional difficulties it is expected that the decision on whether to adopt this basis would be taken with effect from the accounting period in which a group came into being.

EXAMPLE

In the year ended 31st December, 1974, a close parent company receives dividends of £50,000 declared by its subsidiaries for the year ended 31st December, 1973. The parent declares a dividend of £45,000 for the year ended 31st December, 1973, and pays this within a reasonable time after that date (so that the dividend is within the provisions of paragraph 10 (1) (*a*) of Schedule 16 already referred to). If the group adopts the basis described above, the dividends of £50,000 from the subsidiaries will be included in the distributable profits of the parent, for the purposes of determining its distributable profits, for the year ending 31st December, 1973, and not for the year ended 31st December, 1974. (Press Statement, 6th November, 1967.)

4. DISALLOWED DIRECTORS' REMUNERATION

Where directors' remuneration is disallowed for corporation tax purposes the disallowance will not rank as a distribution. Where such a disallowance has been negotiated with the Inspector of Taxes the Schedule E liability of the director will be reduced by the amount of that disallowance, provided that the amount disallowed is formally waived and refunded to the company by the director and a satisfactory settlement, of the amount to be apportioned (if any) under Schedule 16, Finance Act 1972, for that accounting period is reached. (Press Statement 13th July, 1970.)

5. EXCESS OF RELEVANT INCOME OVER DISTRIBUTIONS: SMALL AMOUNTS

Where a close company is a property investment company, or an investment company which is a subsidiary member of a trading group, no apportionment of the excess of the company's relevant income over its distributions will be made for any period in which that excess is not more than £100 (proportionately reduced for accounting periods of less than 12 months.)

(Extra-Statutory Concession C.7.)

NOTES

(*a*) Paragraph 1 (3) of Schedule 16, Finance Act, 1972, exempts from apportionment the income of a trading company, and of an investment company which heads a trading group (within the definition of paragraph 11 (2) (*a*) of that Schedule), unless the excess of relevant income over distributions is more than £1,000. The concession is therefore superseded so far as such companies are concerned but it will continue to apply to property investment companies and investment companies which are subsidiary members of trading groups.

(*b*) Where the property owned by a close investment company is subject to rent control and as a result Schedule A losses arise each year, the company will be regarded as a property investment company provided that the value of the company's assets invested in real property exceeds the value of its other investments. (Press Statement, 13th July, 1970.)

6. Close Companies in Liquidation: Distributions in Respect of Share Capital

It is the practice under the existing system, if the members agree, to treat actual distributions in respect of share capital, out of income of a close company arising after the commencement of a winding-up, as distributions to be charged to income tax (including surtax) to the extent necessary to eliminate a shortfall of distributions. Distributions so treated are not then taken into account for capital gains tax purposes.

Under the new system an excess of relevant income over distributions for an accounting period ending after 5th April, 1973, will not give rise to any basic rate income tax liability and the practice described above will not apply. Where, however, there is such an excess for a period after the commencement of a winding-up and an apportionment is made under the provisions of Schedule 16, Finance Act, 1972, for the purposes of liability to higher rate tax (including investment income surcharge), the resulting liability of a participator will be restricted to the excess, if any, over the capital gains tax he has paid and which he shows is attributable to his receipts (as distributions in respect of share capital) out of the apportioned income for the period.
(Paragraph 107 of the Board's booklet "Corporation Tax", February 1966.)

7. Cessation of Trade and Liquidations

It is the practice to examine cases of reorganisations carried out entirely for bona fide commercial reasons in order to see whether any relaxation of paragraph 13 of Schedule 16, Finance Act, 1972 (apportionment of income on cessation of trade or liquidation) can be given. For this purpose full information about any reorganisation (whether proposed or already carried out) where the point may arise should be given to the Inspector of Taxes when dealing with the tax liabilities of the company or when the question of the application of paragraph 13 to a proposed reorganisation is raised.
(Board's letter 25th July, 1968, to the Accountants' Joint Parliamentary Committee.)

8. Close Companies Owned by Persons Not Resident in the United Kingdom

Where a close company, 90 per cent. or more of the ordinary share capital of which is beneficially owned by non-residents, wishes to retain its surplus funds in this country, a request that the company should not be liable to apportionment of its income will be favourably considered.

(Hansard, 8th February, 1968, vol. 758, No. 56, Written Answers, col. 225.)

9. Cases of Hardship

Sympathetic consideration will be given to the following types of case in which hardship may arise:

(i) Where in computing the profits of a close trading company a relatively large amount of entertaining expenses is disallowed and the income of the company is liable to apportionment based on the maximum relevant income.

(ii) Where a company has made distributions up to its maximum relevant income in an accounting period and the corporation tax profits for that accounting period are reduced because of some factor beyond the company's control.

(iii) Where a company's shares are quoted and dealt in on a recognised stock exchange and for a short period straddling the end of an accounting period the company becomes a close company because during that period less than 35 per cent. of the voting rights were held by the public.

(Press Statement, 13th July, 1970.)

10. Interest on Inter-bank Loans

Where a close company carries on a business of banking and in the normal course of that business borrows money from another bank at the commercial rate of interest appropriate to such a loan, the allowance for corporation tax of interest paid after 15th April, 1969, is not restricted by reference to the limit laid down in Section 285, Income and Corporation Taxes Act, 1970.

(Extra-Statutory Concession C.8 in the Supplement (1971).)

11. Loans to Executors to pay Estate Duty and Capital Gains Tax

Where a close company which is a trading company or a member of a trading group makes a loan to a participator to enable the payment of estate duty the charge to tax under Section 286, Income and Corporation Taxes Act, 1970 (as amended by paragraph 3 of Schedule 17, Finance Act, 1972) is temporarily suspended, subject to the following conditions:

(i) At least one third of the ordinary share capital of the company forms part of the property chargeable to estate duty.

(ii) The loan does not exceed the estate duty which the executors, etc., show could not be paid without realising some or all of the shares in the company on which estate duty is chargeable.

(iii) Estate duty up to the amount of the loan is paid within a short interval (about a month) of the loan being made.

The tax which is suspended becomes chargeable if the loan is not repaid within 5 years of its being made or earlier if in the intervening period condition (ii) ceases to be satisfied.

This concession also applies, subject to the same conditions, to loans to participators to pay capital gains tax arising on death in respect of shares owned by the deceased in the close company at the date of his death and forming part of his estate. (Extra-Statutory Concession C.2 as augmented by Supplement (1971).)

12. CLOSE COMPANIES: LOAN CREDITORS

In applying the test of control of a company in Section 302 (2) (*c*), Income and Corporation Taxes Act, 1970, as amended by paragraph 5 of Schedule 17, Finance Act, 1972, to determine whether or not a company is a close company, a recognised money broker will not be treated as participator of a company carrying on a business as a stock jobber solely by reason of short term loans or advances arising in the ordinary course of their respective trades. (Not previously published.)

2. Memorandum Prepared by the Association of British Chambers of Commerce and the Confederation of British Industries

NOTE:—*Although the Shortfall provisions have been repealed, the considerations relating to the requirements of the business justifying the witholding of dividends are the same. This memorandum is therefore relevant to the definition of "relevant" income for the purposes of statutory apportionment.*

The Confederation of British Industries and the Association of British Chambers of Commerce together have been having discussions with the Inland Revenue about the problems of close companies. One of the main topics was shortfall and its administration. This memorandum has been prepared in the light of these discussions. Copies of the memorandum are being circulated by the Inland Revenue to Inspectors of Taxes as an indication of the views of the C.B.I. and the A.B.C.C. on this topic.

1. The shortfall legislation introduced by the Finance Act, 1965, became effective from 5th April, 1966, and it is only now becoming possible to review how it is working in practice. There is no doubt that the threat of shortfall assessment which overhangs close companies has caused a geat deal of anxiety, especially for the directors of trading companies and their advisers. This memorandum is particularly concerned with trading companies.

2. The principle of the shortfall legislation is not a novelty. Its predecessor, under which a company could be assessed to surtax on its profits if its dividend distributions were unreasonably low, had been in force since 1922. There are, however, two important differences between the old and the new procedures. Under the old procedure the burden of proof was entirely on the Inland Revenue to show that a trading company had not distributed a reasonable proportion of its income. Under the new procedure, it is for the taxpayer to prove that a company could not afford to pay (within certain limits) a larger dividend than it in fact proposes without prejudice to its business requirements.

3. There is also a purely administrative difference. The old system was centrally administered by the Surtax office, in which a relatively

small number of officials were able to accumulate great experience in the handling of this difficult work. The new system is administered by District Inspectors in over 700 different districts.

4. The object of this legislation is to prevent the avoidance of personal taxation that can arise through the agency of a closely controlled company which retains profits in excess of its business requirements. Prior to the 1965 legislation, such retentions could benefit only surtax payers. Under the new system income tax can also be saved by this means but it should be borne in mind that all companies pay corporation tax which is higher than income tax and is not payable by unincorporated traders. There is, therefore, no incentive to use a corporate enterprise to save income tax but, on the contrary, the taxation advantages may well lie with the unincorporated trader except when the proprietors are, or expect to become surtax payers.

5. The declared intention of the corporation tax introduced in 1965 was to encourage the ploughing back of profits for use in the development of a business. It would, therefore, be illogical if close companies, which account for about a quarter of the country's gross national product, were compelled to distribute amounts which ought to be retained to finance the maintenance and development of the business. A close company is, of course, far more dependent on self-financing than a public company, and therefore prudent directors adopt a conservative dividend policy. If profits of say 15 to 20 per cent were earned on capital employed and no dividend at all were paid, companies would be left, after payment of corporation tax, with an annual retention in the region of 9 to 12 per cent on capital employed, which is none too much for an actively expanding business that does not have access to the capital markets. However, the Finance Act, 1965, provides for a maximum distribution of 60 per cent in the case of trading income. Such a dividend, after paying corporation tax, will on the above figures leave only 4 or 5 per cent on capital employed as available for reserves. This is barely enough to maintain the existing business in times of inflation and leaves virtually nothing to finance expansion.

6. There is, therefore, a strong presumption that the great majority of trading companies should be able to adopt the dividend policy suited to their particular needs. It is only those companies which have accumulated cash and liquid resources in excess of their requirements, or those which have used income to repay initial business loans, whose distribution policy can be called in question.

7. While it has been indicated above that the companies with large cash and liquid resources must expect their accounts to be critically examined, it does not follow that higher dividends can necessarily be paid. The onus of proof is, however, then placed upon the company to explain the need for this accumulation of cash and the purpose for which it will ultimately be required.

8. It will be necessary to make some comparison between the future maintenance and development expenditure on the one hand and resources available to meet it on the other. This comparison is not a mere exercise in arithmetic; it must lack precision because it involves forecasting and, in the end, the result is a matter of judgment. As to the

elements of the comparison that is required, maintenance and development expenditure is a wide concept. The company's expenditure plans must be genuine but cannot be precise. A company may intend to build new business premises if it can find land in an appropriate location and obtain planning permission. In such circumstances there is no absolute certainty that the premises can be built within a specified period of time but this would not necessarily invalidate the company's claim to retain funds for this purpose. Again, a company may wish to develop its business by acquiring another business in the same or a related field; provided that the company can show that its intention is genuine and capable of fulfilment it can retain monies to do this.

9. As to the resources which are available to meet any proposed expenditure, it is clear that funds which are invested in fixed assets or current assets of the nature of stock or book debts cannot in most circumstances, be regarded as available for this purpose. So long as the business continues, these assets will not be turned into cash except in unusual circumstances, e.g. where at a particular date either book debts or stock were at an exceptionally high level on account of some special or non-recurring factor. It would, however, only be a very exceptional case in which it could be suggested that a particular level of stock or book debts was not a requirement of the company's business. In a normal case, therefore, the resources which are available, either for the payment of dividends or for future development expenditure, which need to be taken into account in the assessment of a reasonable distribution, are only the liquid assets, i.e. cash or near-cash, such as investments.

10. If a company has no cash or investments, and finances its trading operations by the use of borrowed money such as overdrafts, and this situation is likely to continue, there would seem to be little ground for any shortfall assessment in the normal case.

INDEX